FUNNIER CRYPTO-GRAMS

SHAWN KENNEDY

PUZZLE
WRIGHT
PRESS

New York

**PUZZLE
WRIGHT
PRESS**

New York

An Imprint of Sterling Publishing
1166 Avenue of the Americas
New York, NY 10036

Puzzlewright Press and the distinctive Puzzlewright Press logo
are registered trademarks of Sterling Publishing Co., Inc.

© 2013 by Shawn Kennedy

ISBN 978-1-4549-0005-4

Distributed in Canada by Sterling Publishing
℅ Canadian Manda Group, 664 Annette Street
Toronto, Ontario, Canada M6S 2C8
Distributed in the United Kingdom by GMC Distribution Services
Castle Place, 166 High Street, Lewes, East Sussex, England BN7 1XU
Distributed in Australia by Capricorn Link (Australia) Pty. Ltd.
P.O. Box 704, Windsor, NSW 2756, Australia

For information about custom editions, special sales, and premium and
corporate purchases, please contact Sterling Special Sales at 800-805-5489 or
specialsales@sterlingpublishing.com.

Manufactured in Canada

4   6   8   10   9   7   5   3

www.puzzlewright.com

CONTENTS

INTRODUCTION

Welcome to *Funnier Cryptograms*, a collection of over 400 funny quotes, quips, and one-liners translated into simple substitution codes, to follow up the 370 in my previous book, *Funny Cryptograms*.

If you're new to solving cryptograms, the puzzles can look intimidating. But if you enjoy playing hangman or *Wheel of Fortune*, you can solve cryptograms using the same process of analyzing word patterns and guessing where common letters are located in the puzzle. See the ten solving steps below for a crash course in code breaking.

The puzzles are arranged (approximately) from longer to shorter; shorter usually means harder, but not always. If you'd like a free letter to start you off, look up the puzzle number in the Hints section beginning on page 95. The hint T → E indicates that every T in the code represents the letter E.

Over 400 jokes are waiting for you to decode them, so what are you waiting for? Grab a pencil, and get cracking!

TIPS AND TRICKS FOR SOLVING CRYPTOGRAMS

Each puzzle consists of a quotation followed by the name of its author. Each letter in the original message has been changed to a different letter of the alphabet. No letter represents itself, and substitutions remain consistent throughout each individual puzzle. In the example below, each C represents a U, each X represents an O, each R represents a G, and so on.

L A U G H I N G   O U T   L O U D
E Z C R Y P T R   X C M   E X C Q

Solving relies on trial and error, but these ten steps will help you break into almost any puzzle:

Step 1: Look for one-letter words. These are (almost always) A or I.

Step 2: Look for punctuation marks. Words with apostrophes often end in –'S, –N'T (DON'T, DOESN'T, CAN'T, ISN'T, WON'T), –'D (HE'D, WE'D, YOU'D), –'LL (WE'LL, YOU'LL), –'RE (WE'RE, YOU'RE), and –'VE (I'VE, WE'VE, YOU'VE). A two-letter word with an apostrophe is I'M or I'D; a three-letter word is often IT'S. If a question mark ends a puzzle, its first word is often an interrogative such as IS, DO, DID, CAN, HOW, WHY, WHEN, WHAT, COULD, WOULD, or WHERE. If a comma appears after the first word of a sentence, the word before it could be an adverb that ends –LY. Try OR, AND, or BUT after a mid-sentence comma, and try AND between the last two items in a series of commas.

Step 3: Look for the word THAT. Pattern XYZX is almost always THAT, SAYS, or ELSE. To determine which, see if A appears alone elsewhere in the puzzle, or if the three-letter word THE might appear elsewhere. You can also use that trick to see if pattern XYY is ALL or TOO.

Step 4: Look for THE and AND. If you found A or THAT in the previous steps, THE and AND become even easier to spot. If you suspect a word in the code is THE, count the frequency of its last letter in the overall puzzle. If this letter appears often, there's a good chance it represents E and the word is THE.

Step 5: Note letter frequencies. The most common letters in English are ETAOINSHRDLU, in roughly that order. Letters appearing often are usually vowels, while letters appearing less often are usually consonants.

Step 6: Look for words with rare letter patterns like DID, ALL, TOO, GOING, EVER, EVEN, NEVER, LITTLE, ALWAYS, and PEOPLE. GEORGE is a name that's easy to spot.

Step 7: Look for other common two-letter words like AM, AN, AS, AT, BE, BY, DO, IF, IN, IS, IT, ME, MY, OF, ON, OR, and TO. Two-letter words starting with D, G, and T are always DO, GO, and TO, respectively; ones ending with M, P, and R are always AM, UP, and OR. Keep in mind that in a common two-letter word, one letter is always a vowel, and O is the only vowel that starts and ends two-letter words.

Step 8: Compare short words such as TO and TOO; YOU, YOUR, and YOU'RE; HE, SHE, THE, THEN, THEY, and THEIR; I, IF, IS, IT, IN, and INTO; OF, FOR, and FROM; and so on.

Step 9: Look for repeated letter combinations. These are often TH, HE, IN, ER, AN, RE, ND, AT, and ON. Repeated word endings are often –ER, –ED, and –ING, especially in long words or after a doubled letter. Doubled letters are often LL, NN, SS, and TT; try EE or OO in the center of a four-letter word. Other common word endings to watch for include –LY, –LLY, –ION, and –TION.

Step 10: Use trial and error. If you get stuck, go with your gut and try guessing a letter or two that feels right. Don't forget to rule out impossibilities. In XYZ and AZ, XYZ can't be YOU since no common two-letter word ends with U. And if you've already found the letter T, the pattern ?HE can't be THE (it must be SHE).

Remember there is a Hints section beginning on page 95. Just look up the number of the puzzle you're working on. If you see the hint T → E, then every T in the code represents the letter E.

And if all else fails, sneak a peek at the first word or two of the answer in the back to get yourself started!

—Shawn Kennedy

1. SD UHAMY, S ALZ SDZL M XLDA
MQACFHDZ BSZR ZRH FMD MZ ZRH
QLCXHZZH BRHHX LUHQ BRMZ S
JLDYSNHQHN ZL GH MD LNN DCFGHQ.

                    —YZHUHD BQSARZ

2. VH LOSPGVS YFSOFDG MSUBEPL CEAD
VEUDY S GSH MTDP YTD MSY YEKFH.
YTD'Y PEPDFH-YDADP PWM, SPG MD GWP'F
BPWM MTDOD FTD TDUU YTD EY.

                    —DUUDP GDLDPDODY

3. QL Z VCN NETTR HCE CSWJ ZDY ZRGR
FCA LZRP HCE AWJW KCQDK, Z KCCY
PFQDK PC RZH QR, "Q YCD'P GDCA, Q AZR
RNWWYQDK PFW AFCTW PQBW."

                    —UZVG FZDYWH

4. VB'Z PKUR LQU BPT CQRTUA
MTATUKBVQA BQ HARTUZBKAR BPQUTKH,
GPQ SVJTR NTZVRT K DQAR NHB RVRA'B
QGA GKBTU ZXVZ QU K ZAQUXTS.

                    —NVSS JKHMPKA

5. LEJ YDX VDL DXL CEEFPVO AOPXK AE
D ZEK, DXZ OB SPFF KPGB LEJ D FEER
FPRB, "TL KEZ, LEJ'UB UPKOA! P XBGBU
SEJFZ'GB AOEJKOA EC AODA!"

                    —ZDGB HDUUL

36. FCZLWR GA NMCE C QAAGWAGM
NMJMVOUMJ FCZLWR GA RA EASWJGCLNJ
GA CWJSMN GFM EAAN SFLUM LW GFM
VLEJG AQ VCTLWR UAZM. —WAMU BASCNE

37. HTOK TG UCTUHC ZFMO OT WRAC
ZRON JTX RM ONC HRDT. ZNFO JTX ZFMO
RK KTDCTMC ZNT ZRHH OFBC ONC PXK
ZRON JTX ZNCM ONC HRDT PWCFBK ATZM.
—TUWFN ZRMGWCJ

38. O ZXV PDY PQ X GXYB FBEBQYAH XQG
YLB JDH YPPR WB LPFVBCXER FOGOQJ.
YLXY ZXV ROQG PK KDQ, DQYOA ZB FXQ
PDY PK MDXFYBFV. —VDVOB APDERV

39. KCE VCSP EKPU ACZ GRCE JU D MCF'Y
LDVP, KP FPOY SDM DO ACZ, GZO EKPU
ACZ ODQP KJS JU D VDX, KP YOJVQY KJY
KPDM CZO OKP EJUMCE?
—YOPBP GRZPYOPJU

40. BUSXMAXDX UC QAHB KRUYX, XTXDL
QXC BXZUCOB, QAXDX HB W MUSWC
KHTHCK YHDQA QU W ZAHRO. BAX SEBQ YX
JUECO WCO BQUVVXO. —BWS RXTXCBUC

41. NRDP J WJG J LRVB JGO BP KRUU PJE
LXQ J OJF. EPJMB BRW BXK EX LRVB, JGO
BP KRUU VRE RG J AXJE JGO OQRGT APPQ
JUU OJF. —NPXQNP MJQURG

42. SU HWH OWTH, "SWNNU W KTNG BYL
YWO PYX OWSX CXGTXA WO PYX AWSTGU."
BYU BLQGH T BWJP PL SWNNU OLSXLJX
BYL PYTJVO T'S W OEYSQEV?
—WHWS OWJHGXN

43. KYXSFBXSK B GYMCSL BT XSM NMC
GYXSM LSNWWQ KZBF SNDU YFUSL.
JSLUNJK FUSQ KUYZWC WBAS MSPF CYYL
NMC EZKF ABKBF MYG NMC FUSM.
—VNFUNLBMS USJHZLM

44. Y FOQDXU DV GX DRX EYAMD FVPOQ
DV GKAQ RXA GAO, GKD YD FVKHU RONX
DOBXQ DRX EYAX UXZOADPXQD EVKA UOTM
DV ZKD YD VKD. —UVHHT ZOADVQ

45. LKVPBWIHU SKWDH WB PDHKWSP
ZPGHY WB LFHK MLKZA QWOOWLB
ULOOPKY P AHPK PBU YRHBUY FHKA
OWZZOH LB LMMWSH YERROWHY.
—TLLUA POOHB

46. L GO EHYZNKSX WU MJS BJDGKS
"KMHB, XDHB, GYX DHFF." MJS "KMHB"
BGDM XHSKY'M WSFHYV. MJGM'K PNKM
SRMDG MLOS ZHD WSLYV HY ZLDS.

       —PHY ZDLSXOGY

47. HUZUZQUH JWPJ PL P JUUAPVUH, ORE
PHU PJ JWU YPLJ LJPVU RK OREH YXKU
FWUA ORE FXYY QU WPGGO JR WUPH JWU
GWRAU XL KRH ORE.   —KHPA YUQRFXJI

48. RFOOUQ OEOY'K LSK GQTTESO
RSMQFHS UEH DEBS DPFAO UQCS HQEO,
"DUQK, QTS JPF LPEYL KP HEK QTPFYO
AEXS KUQK QAA OQJ?"

       —LQTTJ HUQYOAEYL

49. DO ENL AY OQPY OBNO LHP TNJ'O
ZHHS NSS OBY KYHKSY NSS OBY ODEY,
APO LHP TNJ ZHHS YJHPXB HZ OBYE OH
QPSY N SNQXY THPJOQL. —CDSS WPQNJO

50. NCZHPCEA SCZFYQZHKOHE ZH CK ZA
EGQJQKU OCELA. OVHA YHTO L KCOH CK
OVH BQKENVQHYE OVLO NLQE, "FLGXQKU
TQKH."   —OCZZA SCCFHG

51. VDE LPD MZVJKD. QODN WLE MSPUZUD L BOAKD BDDGDEC BZQO FSMQ QOPDD QOZEYM: TDDP, TAHDP MOAPQM, LEC TLQQDPZDM XAP QOD PDVAQD WAEQPAK.

— CZLEL FAPCLE

52. QRZXVZ WZNGWA NJHV YCCL. H MHAS NJXN NJCGEJ FP MWHZASV XWZ QCCW XWHNJFZNHKHXAV, NJZP XWZ AZXWRP XRR ECCS YCCLLZZQZWV.

— VHW TXRNZW VKCNN

53. J VFFP HUBBX VUB AFUAPF NSU ZUR'K ZBJRC. NSFR KSFX NOCF DA JR KSF QUBRJRT, KSOK'H OH TUUZ OH KSFX'BF TUJRT KU VFFP OPP ZOX.

— VBORC HJROKBO

54. SHXOYHB CVGY NYXFOHYN JYXSKEY OB MSN S EYHSBY. HVU UMSB'E DVOHD BV MSRRYH BV KE UOBM JVBM S EYHSBY SHN S MVKEY?

— UOFF CVDYCE

55. Q MGBZ BWMZPCQPZ'O YWU. TNZP UGK'EZ W RQY, ZBZEUGPZ FZCO W BWMZPCQPZ. QC'O MQRZ, "CG CQH: PQXZ LWPCO. MGBZ OXGCC."

— HQRZ SQESQFMQW

77. Y RVXME HB VCP OYRCHBZVFB GFRV
RYER OFAPB CYLP WPVVPJ LPJWYU
RTHUUR VCYB APB. VF VCP YXVCFJR FQ
VCYV RVXME: MXC!   —DFBYB F'WJHPB

78. NRHU TRHLSGUEF PEU TPCCUJ RO
GR LUEVREH HPOZ OUQ VSOTGDROF,
DOTCSJDOA TROFSHLGDRO RV NRHUQREM
VREHUECZ UPGUO KZ GNU JRA.
                          —JRSA CPEFRO

79. EHVVALHHR MF EMKE FBEHHV. WG
PBWHDF PDS TDSFEYSZ, BHYSRA PBWHDF
PDS OCZMHDF, PZR RDPYPWMB PBWHDF
PDS WES BHHV FSZMHDF.   —HLSZ LMVFHZ

80. F DHEJX BZFH YNV FS ZJ ZDX BZJ
BFAJ. ZJ HDFX ZJ'X CMLJ BM YFLJ FB BM
AJ, PNB ZJ TDHK'B HNGJ ZJ QMNCX ADEJ
BZJ QMAAFBAJKB.   —QDGMC HFHEFKX

81. CWQWV DVM DK JFLVWNN Y UKFYC
TWSYRNW JZ MKR BK, NPW'AA WGLWSD
MKR DK OWWL RL DK DPW NDYCBYVB ZKV
DPW VWND KZ MKRV AJZW.   —U.S. ZJWABN

21

82. OGRRJWR JF BNYV MNWNKJSJDA. JQ'F
RGGC KGY VGZY ANRF DWC VGZY KNNQ,
DWC DAFG QTN RYGZWC. JQ EDUNF JQ
KNNA WNNCNC.   —STDYANF FSTZAI

83. KLO FEWC GNE BLF SY KXZWC QXOO
SY KLO FEO BLF MNE KZXE HFBE NE
SEPSKNKSFE KF HSEEOX BSKLFZK RSPSER
NE OAMZYO.   —TZWOY XOENXH

84. N BRABKY LBFQ ZUWCMRQ
UQTQTMQUNVE ZLUQQ ZLNVEY: DBOQY,
VBTQY, BVH N OBV'Z UQTQTMQU ALBZ ZLQ
ZLNUH ZLNVE NY.   —DUQH BRRQV

85. HKX AXLZ GXBLTX LSERH VXLZOBY
FOHK L NODX-MXLA-EZV OC HKLH OB BE
HOGX LH LZZ MER SXYOB HE CERBV ZOWX
L NODX-MXLA-EZV.   —QXLB WXAA

86. UDPWXEJ ADGGTLP NEJPXSTLDMBQ
AELT GWDJ WELEPNECTP, LDGWTL AELT
GWDJ SEV PWEOP, DJS PBXVWGBQ AELT
GWDJ WENZTQ.   —LEQ MBEHJG YL.

87. WKS EBJJSZW ZSXXSP BZ AQQVEQQVZ
UDN WKS ZSAQDN BZ NBSW EQQVZ —
KQH DQW WQ SUW HKUW CQM'GS TMZW
XSUPDSN KQH WQ AQQV.   —UDNC PQQDSC

88. AY UOV VZKRATO RFZKWFKV XFNV FZL TVZTV, "RFJPFNFATAJFR" SCWRN OFQV TCXVUOAZK UC NC SAUO F TOCEUFKV CY YRCSVET.   — NCWK RFETCZ

89. A GHLY VUKST MURY UV WGY JYMW FYHMUSM A YLYF GHT VUF FYRHASASZ HW WGY JUWWUR MARXEP JP EUUQASZ HW WGY RYS HW WGY WUX.   — VFHSQ RUUFY BUEJP

90. PMK LKFJGC TGZKC VGC'P HYFE QGGPAFYY DJ AKNFBJK KYKRKC GQ PMKZ TGBYV CKRKL TKFL PMK JFZK GBPQDP DC HBAYDN.   — HMEYYDJ VDYYKL

91. GLW YUTDLG XGGWRMXRG OTUU XUOXFE GWUU FZJ GLW RXBW ZY FZJC VTUZG. UTQW XRFZRW DZWE, "ZL, LW'E DZZM. T UTQW LTE OZCQ."   — MXKTM EVXMW

92. HCAAZWU JK MJNA ZCJTN. JH EWB FPNA PTE PF PMM, EWB UJQGF PK OAMM FPNA ATWBQG FW UPNA EWB GPXXE HWC P OGJMA.   — HJTMAE XAFAC ZBTTA

93. C DECVJ ZS TEBKMY WKTD DCF DES
PBXSOVGSVD CL CD YBST N PBBY WBR.
LCLDSSV FSOUSVD CT DES TDNVYNOY DCF,
CTV'D CD?   —FND FNKMTSV

94. LKOAY JP VYS LCKBBYAV TDB'J
YSQKBT DHU CDUFIDBV, TDB'J XKMY HV
OYJJYU QYDQAY, KBT TDB'J LDXY FB
LAYKUAW YBDHZC.   —OFAA XKCYU

95. H ZVPWF FKCZO DHAE QVP AHWW AEO
ZVDX ZVSO EVSO. VC XOZVCF AEVPBEA,
H'WW FKCZO DHAE AEO ZVDX AHWW QVP
ZVSO EVSO.   —BUVPZEV SKUG

96. MTOKPFDVGBTO EPGLPPO VWVN VOW
PKP NJDG XVKP EPPO WBRRBMJQG VG
GBNPD EPMVJDP GXPH XVW OTETWH GT
GVQC VETJG.   —VSOPD FPYYQBPF

97. SCPUZBWZR PCWEL QAWQ WERUEC
ZWE VBUN DO QU XC OBCLKSCEQ, WES
WERUEC NAU SUCLE'Q VBUN DO ZWE XC
JKZC OBCLKSCEQ.   —YUAEER ZWBLUE

98. A ZSHW XDRCU QZW PWLQ MSO QD
YAHW SUHATW QD NO TZAFUJWC AL QD
XACU DRQ MZSQ QZWO MSCQ QD UD QZWC
SUHALW QZWN QD UD AQ.
                          —ZSJJO L. QJRNSC

24

99. FSV EQ EB BFZB SHD RZBAF AZH
QBZPB Z OSPDQB OEPD, WDB EB BZCDQ
Z VFSND YSG SO RZBAFDQ BS QBZPB Z
AZRMOEPD?   —AFPEQBW VFEBDFDZJ

100. GVZGMV RXYTB ZW RXV YTDVTRZJ KQ
K QFJVANKMM, NHR TZ ZTV VDVJ KQBQ
RXV YTDVTRZJ AXKR XV RXYTBQ ZW ZRXVJ
GVZGMV.   —FXKJMVQ W. BVRRVJYTP

101. EM TKQFPH BZKKM QN QP AZQB
PVS. DF JVY YSFPYM-TQCF MFZKN TVK
NVEFYDQPJ DF HQHP'Y HV. DF HQHP'Y KOP
TZNY FPVOJD.   —HZEVP SZMZPN

102. LR W QSEVBWRX NZWMB,
WMYSWZEJEHLBQB FLJJ XLH VA QWRRLRH
CZXB WRX QSLRG FZ TMLZX AZEAJZ WB
AVRLBSUZRQ.   —EJLOLW FLJXZ

103. QUVYSGC'Z CUU YSEJB SQ MVH DCR
TPPW QYVO DCBDJSRE C ZCSUQSZJ CRG
EVSRE BV BJP PAWPRZP VQ JCFSRE SB
OVHRBPG.   —TSR JHKKCYG

104. HT NAL WZAG NALP CHCYS QZR NALP
OEQWSODSQPS QZR JQZ OEAAB JPQDO,
NAL EQKS Q YHCSPQY SRLJQBHAZ.
          —BQYYLYQE CQZWESQR

105. VXCLUXE QDEXSCHL QDE LDFJPUL:
WCEY. SDFLJFOXW WCEY DTXEFJPUL, VJLU
VJWXZK HSCLLXEXW ZJPUL GK BDEFJFP.

                                    —PXDEPX SCEZJF

106. E QEGH EO VXOKLV LXFD ON SNVOVXD
X YBFEGLFFRXG. YLEGJ YPXGH, VXOKLV
ZVBLP, XGH EGZNRSLOLGO ZNRLF
GXOBVXPPD ON RL.   —MNKG ZPLLFL

107. JSRNGVAE YVA XBYVCAV CSYE YEP
QD FX. MEQK SQK R MEQK? R GQE'C MEQK
QEA JSRNG KRCS Y DFNN-CRBA LQZ YEG
JSRNGVAE.   —ZRNN SRJMX

108. VRLHD FCBXKP BM YKPPHUQL BCYBXL
EKVHUPL VK AJ MSK VRLHD FCBXKP
JAE LACPHKEL OKJAEK MSKX QA HUMA
OBMMCK.   —SKHUEHDS SKHUK

109. F JUER RP B YUZPYH GNPW BEH
GBFH, "JNBR NBCU APT SPR QA RNU
HPPYG?" NU GBFH, "B QTZOUR PX GBEH
BEH B XFYU QVBEOUR."   —RFD CFEU

110. BXRT F QFT XFV F KEJWXLFH, XR
WFZRV F LFH MDD. BXRT F BMQFT XFV F
KEJWXLFH, VXR WFZRV FW PRFVW WXJRR
HRFJV MDD.   —YMFT JEURJV

26

111. NXW'F NX JWPFOSWE QSHHP HSVA
EXSWE XBFQSNA NBZSWE J OBZZSMJWA FX
OJKA QAL. FAHH PXBZ DZSAWNQ PXB NSN,
RBF NXW'F. — NZ. ZBFO

112. KVAVQ JV TNQTYU OM BTRWX TO
CMRQEVBN. TNOVQ TBB, CMR DMRBU
JV LYEEYKW MRO MK OXV ZMGV MN OXV
DVKORQC. — UTLV VUKT VAVQTWV

113. XPJNY YBTFHXQ ATQYHB YNTG QEZGR.
YNPQ PQ LNM QEDH SHESXH TSSHTB
CBPJNY ZGYPX MEZ NHTB YNHD QSHTV.
— TXTG RZGRHQ

114. UAC EWJJCPCMDC TCUBCCM S USH
DFZZCDUFP SME S USHWECPKWQU WQ
UASU UAC USHWECPKWQU USYCQ FMZG
GFNP QYWM. — KSPY UBSWM

115. MYVJV PJV MYJVV NPLE MG UVM
EGXVMYCHU SGHV: SG CM LGBJEVTW,
VXATGL EGXVGHV, GJ WGJQCS LGBJ
RYCTSJVH MG SG CM. — XGHMP RJPHV

116. W'E QGKPHSOVO RF LVPLDV BYP BQSK
KP "CSPB" KYV HSWTVNGV BYVS WK'G
YQNO VSPHAY KP XWSO FPHN BQF QNPHSO
UYWSQKPBS. — BPPOF QDDVS

117. GDTCXMG XO QWT MKJRQCL HWTCT LKJ MGR NJL G ZXUTQXDT OJAAZL KU GOAXCXR UKC G PKZZGC GRP JOT XQ JA XR QHK HTTYO. —VKWR NGCCLDKCT

118. NL ELAOZZOVAGNZ EP PSHOSLO JCS VNL ZEPAOL AS ACO "JEZZENH AOZZ" SROMAGMO NLX LSA ACELU SW ACO ZSLO MNLKOM. —TEZZD VSLLSZZD

119. HPFK JWG ZFTRP BWZ EPF QETZQ, JWG DTJ KWE YGSEF OFE WKF, CGE JWG HWK'E RWDF GX HSEP T PTKABGV WB DGA FSEPFZ. —VFW CGZKFEE

120. UOV HWVDHBV QHC XOL TLVG CLU MCLX XOHU UL TL XEUO OEG NEYV XHCUG HCLUOVD LCV XOERO XENN NHGU YLDVWVD. —HCHULNV YDHCRV

121. C EVXY YU YRV YRCDYCVYR DVMXCUX UJ KS WDVQHRUUP. C OCOX'Y ENXY YU BU GVHNMQV C'ZV WMY UX PCAV N RMXODVO WUMXOQ. —EVXOS PCVGKNX

122. XR JFVNFO ENHHOEKM VNZH THNFZFEXJKXNF NR J ANHC XF J TZQDXE TDJEO, VNZ PJGO OGOHV HXWPK KN TZFEP PXB XF KPO FNMO. —POVANNC QHNZF

123. MEFK FK AG QOMFATMY UTSMTKG:
PTMBEFSV CNB PFME T BHYXFM BTHX
PEFOY ATDFSV ORNY TSX YTMFSV TM MEY
KTAY MFAY.   —GTKAFSY LOYYME

124. VPTO EDOOZDMY ZK ZJ SOPTWBY
ZG VPTO LZGY KDVK, "VPT'OY PJBV
ZJSYOYKSYN ZJ PJY SRZJM," DJN VPT
XDJ'S OYEYEWYO LRDS ZS ZK.
                       —EZBSPJ WYOBY

125. NS BMVFRPA UNFEOPU RNK LFZ
SLNRC HPMRO L KOKMNP LXMVR KLPPNOZ
DNSO, HMVDZ RCOA WVXDNUC NR
RCPMVEC KBEPLH-CNDD?
                       —UCLHF QOFFOZA

126. URUYTGPBT LQ F XUMLOQ. GOS LW
TPO COBXU F WLQZ GT LSQ FGLKLST SP
NKLJG F SYUU, LS ALKK KLRU LSQ AZPKU
KLWU GUKLURLMX LS LQ QSODLB.
                       —FKGUYS ULMQSULM

127. YE NEBJZ SC HREZ VYQ Y BJSVE CSL
KDZ LREPJREP MLSKDZLQ BRLBNQ. VDZE
DZ FRZF, YJJ DRQ CLRZEFQ VZEK KS KDZ
CNEZLYJ RE SEZ BYL.   —QKZTZE VLRPDK

29

128. E WXKQB FNZBNZY BNZ FXYSW NXSWA
PXY MVGXVZ M TXYZ AXKS-ABEYYEVL
AKYJYEAZ BNMV BNZ PEYAB ZUJZYEZVDZ
FEBN EDZ DYZMT.   —NZGFXXW QYXKV

129. ZAJEVLY EZN AJXSFJ VJ TVRN DSRVLY
TABN EA S OADSL. VE'J JADNEZVLY V ALTC
YNE EA HA OZNL WVTTC XFCJEST TNSBNJ
EAOL.   —JENBN DSFEVL

130. EB FO XPHXQEXBVX, EY OKC DGSX
MK RXXH MDX UGSGMKQO WKKQ TDCM
JO XPMXBWEBZ OKCQ UXYM UXZ, EM'T
FKWXQB GQVDEMXVMCQX.
                    —BGBVO JGBRT-TFEMD

131. OTKKQUO WU QZTW GBHJCZ DT CQYT
GQKKQUO ZHLU HU W FQU; QK GBHJCZ
PWYT SHJ VJPF JF WUZ LWUK KH ZH
GHPTKBQUO.   —T.C. GQPFGHU

132. R QCJWETJJVRE ETTLJ MGOTT
CVQOTDDRJ: UET MU DTRBT RM GUVT, UET
MU DTRBT RM MGT UXXWST, REL UET MU
DTRBT UE MGT MORWE.   —FRCD LWSZJUE

133. S VBSTA GSQORRV SL GPWFFD.
VBEV'L VBM UFRGPMJ. VBMFM'L E PEFQM,
RWV-RO-ORHWL JRTLVMF FREJSTQ VBM
HRWTVFDLSKM.   —JSVHB BMKGMFQ

145. BM MOW BHW NX XNQC FTMO YBYWC OBMR BVP FNNPWV RFNCPR, FW'CW BZZ HWVVCBZR. NVZD RNAW NX QR VWEWC HCNF NQM NX TM. — YWMWC QRMTVNE

146. G TDUFFM OJNC FDM FX KFBM GW B NXWKFBWF KFBFU XQ NXWQJKGXW AJKF PUNBJKU XQ FCU USTDUKKGXW GF EUBHUK XW OM QBNU. — AXCWWM VUTT

147. VASBAM EVA CB VAS VGBJAO BU LBQW HQBFPCMC PO PDA'O ONM LBQW NM PD DJHHBDMC OB YM CBPAR VO ONVO GBGMAO. — QBYMQO YMAENZMS

148. VFP EGK HFM NWBPWVPL VFP QNZUV HFPPX HCU CW NLNMV. VFP EGK HFM NWBPWVPL VFP MVFPZ VFZPP, FP HCU C EPWNGU. — UNL OCPUCZ

149. NYMECMO CH RAMNDXKGB PXYCMCMO KAX OCXBH. CP'H PFD KCXHP RYW PFDW BDYXM PA OGDHH RFYP Y QYM CH OACMO PA NA ZDKAXD FD NADH CP. — EFXCHPALFDX QAXBDW

150. X PTDK KM SM MD KVU IUWMIJ TDJ ETL X VTOU DUOUI GIXDTKUJ XD FGHZXW. HGK KVU DXSVK XE EKXZZ LMGDS. — TRL FMUVZUI

33

151. RZYC U FYN V ZYVXVBZY, U XD RZVN
UN MVOM DC NZY VMTULUC WDNNGY: NVEY
NRD VCX EYYT VRVO PLDH BZUGXLYC.

— LDMYVCCY WVLL

152. PA DJUABYQ FOAW GEY FJQV EW
JW EUSAWCJQ DJURAC PADJYXA GEY'UA
XCARRSWH EW XENAPELG'X RXGDOALAQSD
ZSXSEW. — CSNECOG QAJUG

153. B KEPQ GU DEX. HZKK, B JAEH HSZOZ
GU DEX BP. BQ'P DVPQ QSWQ HSZA B CE
QSZOZ, QSZOZ'P QSBP AZH CVU YEBAC
BQ. — XEXRWQ CEKYQSHWBQ

154. XCDTPWJADF DJ UECP SN NASN
LELTPN QATP EPT FTCJEP JSRJ NE
SPENATC, "QASN! REO NEE? D NAEOZAN D
QSJ NAT EPMR EPT!" — V.J. MTQDJ

155. ZXA QXSMFC ZO VKUO QOB KCYENO
PGST VXO JSJO? EP XO URSZQ KRAVXERW
KLSMV EV, XO QXSMFCR'V.

— WOSGWO LOGRKGC QXKZ

156. WN JPAFYKT XMYBUXEQQN VYTUB
UPEAC M RMN, NPE OMN VGVKBEMQQN TVB
BP WV M WPCC MKR JPAF BJVQGV UPEAC
M RMN. — APWVAB XAPCB

157. V'W JAA VH UJMXC XU NYYZVHF
KJHFYCXLD RYJZXHD XLQ XU QPY
PJHKD XU UXXAD. AYQ'D DQJCQ RVQP
QTZYRCVQYCD.   —UCJHN AAXTK RCVFPQ

158. LZ MYKWPLCDJQY TR CFQY QTMJDZ
KWP RDTAA PCQRW'D WQQP MAKRRQR.
RJQ PYTWVR YTMJD CBD CS DJQ OCDDAQ.
               —JQWWZ ZCBWMLKW

159. XKYM K XKY UKO TKWWRY VY WNPR
ZVLU K DVEW VY K WVDUL ON QVX UR
ZNSWQ YNL UKPR JUNORY K OSVL HM VL.
               —XKSEVJR JURPKWVRE

160. XNJQM, VX XQYOP CNHO LHQVFP
QFJ OAANHX XN CQYO NWX XSO VFDNCO-
XQK ANHC XSQF VX JNOP XN CQYO XSO
VFDNCO.   —QBAHOJ O. FOWCQF

161. DJGOG PN KAQV KAG PXXHDETQG QEZ
PA QPBG: PA E CGADQGXEA'N DKPQGD,
PALKXPAC DOEBBPL JEN DJG OPCJD KB
ZEV.   —JHCJ QGKAEOW

162. PNJNFBENO NG HAB CNVGH FTOKB N
DU PABL N'S TUUJNLD CUV JLUPTBEDB —
UV PABL N POLH HU KVBOHB GUSB.
               —GHBFABL KUTWBVH

163. QRXCQKVZQVRF: Q AFNYWV GJWP GF
LVWG GFHH FVWCUJ ZW SWNNWG DNWP,
SCZ VWZ GFHH FVWCUJ ZW HFVT ZW.

— QPSNWYF SKFNRF

164. U FAL LSBBRJ HR AQRK UEJ GUPJ,
"JPJE'O DAS GRR OWR GOAL GPTE?" P
GUPJ, "DRUW, CSO P JAE'O CRBPRQR
RQRKDOWPET P KRUJ." — GORQRE NKPTWO

165. OGH FJWZKT U AGZ GL BGYKHQ. ZMK
ZJGPEAK WT, MK'T TZPBV FWZM TG YURQ
EUH UBZGJT FMG HGR'Z VRGF MGF ZG
XAUQ LPRRQ. — OUJJWTGR VKWAAGJ

166. F PMYA FX KBAJ F BZYA Z
JFQBXSZUA. XM SA, XBZX SAZJW F QMX
SV SMJAV'W KMUXB MCX ML XBMWA AFQBX
BMCUW. — RZSAW GZSAUMJ

167. GOG PTX CDHW HKTXV VCD BDFFTZ
ZCT KFHJDG HWOVCJDVOQ BTW COU
GOYTWQD? COU ZOBD RXV VZT HSG VZT
VTLDVCDW. — DHWF ZOFUTS

168. JAGW KQKBF LJZZYY OQJTKHYB KA
C BKAEGY EGCBB CGG ZJSQ YBBYARKCG
ZJJH EQJSOB: CGLJFJG, LCZZYKAY,
BSECQ, CAH ZCR. — CGYV GYTKAY

169. WAQPE LPQNV PN VKT GWJ DAUS
XKPZK XT WQT QTBPSGTG XKWV XT WQT
US VKT UVKTQ VKQTT KDSGQTG WSG
NPOVJ-LUDQ. — BWQH VXWPS

170. QEQ PZJ RKRC GRR HVOH DOEYHEYA,
HVR "XZYO SEGO"? EH OSLOPG CRXEYQG
XR ZU O CRDZCHRC SEGHRYEYA HZ O
DZSEHENEOY. — CZFRCH ZCFRY

171. HXGGXTV XG S WUSTG YE VUDDXTV
DQY BUYBMU GY PMYGU DYVUDKUL DKSD
DKUR PST'D GUU STRDKXTV QLYTV QXDK
USPK YDKUL. — LUTU RSGUTUH

172. AL OWUBV QTV GJB OWQHS, OB
OWKHSV'G JTNB OTQX — CKXG AVGBVXB
VBZWGATGAWVX BNBQR GOBVGR-BAZJG
STRX. — QWYAV OAHHATUX

173. OXFFGB UYB XN TLBE MSP'QB OBR NS
OUEM DBSDGB RLUR BQBCM EBT DBCNSE
MSP OBBR CBOXEFN MSP SH NSOBSEB
BGNB. — SYFBE EUNL

174. X CGQMWAXP TXFS GU MWS NJYP
BNNA PNR TXJ CYNK NJ XJA ULGM NJ XJA
SESQPCNAP QRUWSU MN HSM X LGSTS.
— CNCCP FSYMNJ

175. UDLKPJV DYO NDOF UDLKPJV ZJDYO
BAJ DZ JVP ZATQPUP JFTP BR DNN JVDJ D
VBZJ DYO VBZJPZZ ZVBANO YBJ KP.

— UDC KPPQKBVU

176. ZFO UCFM YKSWS'X E GWFHPSA MQYK
YKS SLOJEYQFC XZXYSA MKSC FCPZ FCS
FT YKS YKWSS W'X HSDQCX MQYK W.

— LSCCQX AQPPSW

177. NEXS RTV'BX LEFBLR, RTV'BX TQC
XSTVDE LT WSTN MXLLXB, MVL ALFQQ
RTVSD XSTVDE LT DT UEXUC USC CT FL.

— MBFDFLLX MUBCTL

178. GJKZ CEYKEZK AHQKC AE JUZS YK
U TXQKH, QA'C BQZS ET XQBK AJKN'HK
CUNQZV, "JKHK, NED AJHEG AJQC UGUN."

— YQAMJ JKSWKHV

179. O YTBP XQ NQEABXB OS TAQKXT,
CSP XUBS O KBCGOIBP LQY NCS
JYL XKQAUOBT. SQD O'E RQQP CX
BZBKLXUOSR.   — PBEBXKO ECKXOS

180. YK PHOVJ AG, AIJE IHGJ H MJHAIJZ
PIHKKJV. AMJKAE-SYRZ IYRZC YS MJHAIJZ.
MJ IHW CYXJAIBKD VBUJ AIHA MIJZJ B
DZJM RF. MJ PHVVJW BA H MBKWYM.

— WHK CFJKPJZ

38

181. ESKV L'J VBM LV G XKCGMLBVYSLO,
L YSGZK BVK CKR. MSGM EGU ESKV L
YCKKO, LM QKKCY CLNK L'J ELMS G
EBJGV.　　　　　—RGXXU YSGVHCLVR

182. KQSZS CZS NJUH KQZSS EKCASE DNZ
C BNGCJ TJ QNUUHBNNP: RCRS, PTEKZTFK
CKKNZJSH, CJP "PZTMTJA GTEE PCTEH."
　　　　　　　　　—ANUPTS QCBJ

183. D XKUV KRAKCG RDFVQ ZRQVE SVY.
OXVC KEV NTGO SZEV KOOEKMODUV OZ
SV. ZJ MZTEGV, KO SC KWV, OXVEV KEVY'O
SKYC RVJO.　　　　　—HVOOC AXDOV

184. TZYKDGX TGW CZPEWP QU XYGTVEW
OTLGBOBDZX GZNWX. YKW EGWTY DVWX
TGW YKDZEKY STP, YKW XSTNN DVWX
JDDNX.　　　　　—TNWMTVPWG LDLW

185. ONBKS BK ZWN FXHV BY JBGN ONBKS
BK OQV YLQAZY, NRLNDZ ZWFZ ZWN OQV
YLQAZY WFCN FMAJZ YADNXCBYBQK.
　　　　　　　　　—OJFGN LJFXG

186. ORBGB'H ZCORTZJ PCF ELZ GBLWWP
NC OC MGBMLGB OC GCEU. NC PCF
MGBMLGB OC BLO L NBWTETCFH VBLW?
LGB PCF RFZJGP? ORBZ PCF'GB JCZZL
BLO TO.　　　　　—ALEU IWLEU

187. KEKZP UBX SJ B ABUX CYYW CYZ
BG WKBJG CSEK USXNGKJ B ABP. DSJAYU
HYXJSJGJ SX XYG KOHKKASXQ GRK
WSUSG.   —KWFKZG RNFFBZA

188. KM TKC KM X'D BPGBLCGLH, "JUPD"
XM K JPCH YUKY JKM XGOLGYLH YP DKVL
LOLCRPGL MPWGH FXVL K EWYFLC.
                         —BKFOXG YCXFFXG

189. ZX HS, ZOS XEZNXXJU PU BOGZ FXE
HEUZ YGUU ZOJXELO PW XJNSJ ZX LSZ
AJXH FXEJ GYGJZHSWZ ZX FXEJ ZGDPRGQ.
                         —AJGW CSQXBPZI

190. GL WSYSQ RFC RL CSQ ASRADS
WFLLST LTRK BSKRTTBRGHW, HRSW CBVC
KSVQ CBVC CBS RCBST CBTSS ASRADS
SQNRM CBSK?   —WVD HVYGQR

191. ESXLX FC ZJCE DKX ESFKB F VQK
RLDHFCX ODJ QUDJE ESX DJEXL CRQVX
RLDBLQH: ODJL EQG WDNNQL AFNN BD
YQLESXL.   —AXLKSXL MDK ULQJK

192. BN UYG ZYXHAJ ZTAJA UYGJ RTBCH
CANV TBQ JYCCAJ QPFVAQ, VJU ZFCPBXS
FJYGXH VTA TYGQA BX VTA HFJP.
                         —CAYLYCH NARTVXAJ

193. SET KWDQ G SWLGP SWHC ZDP TDGHQ
ZW MEGPXD G LGP, ZEDP MWLRAGYP ED'Q
PWZ ZED LGP QED LGHHYDK?

—JGHJHG QZHDYQGPK

194. GTVV PN WF GTKYBPER NRTNYX PX
VYN TXSRVRN, UTEOCPXS ECR JPBQN
OCTXSR OYVYB TXQ GTVV GBYW ECR
EBRRN.   —QTKPQ VREERBWTX

195. J'T ZBDT FYXYKY, LD AUYXCLRJNJXR
AD TP JL HGLA AUGBLKYW OJAU TDBP
ZDDK. YXK J'T AUYXCZGM ZDB AUYA.

—UDOJP TYXKPM

196. PS JNSWZAVRT MHQ BDVHKARU
NR PV MAKD DAQ QVBZVKHZS. A WNXRT
CAOQKABG NR DAQ BNCCHZ, BNLVZVT
MAKD MAKV-NXK.   —MVRTS CAVJPHR

197. EQM EKA WMLJBSO CMYBHMD UAC
DTYYMDD LCM XTBWJBSO L XMEEMC
ZATDMECLH LSJ UBSJBSO L XBOOMC
WAAHQAWM.   —MJOLC L. DQALUU

198. SK WXKKSB, WQX ROOSTW HZMXB
REZCW R QRPO PXTWRKDAX RKO BXXFB WZ
RHECBQ R NCIIG ERAA YSWQ R HZOSNSXO
BKZYBQZX.   —XAASZW TQRIX

199. M GZAR EU VZKGC OVMG PCCD. M
TZO Q WFCOOU TZZR WFMBC SZF MO, JKO
MO EQRC EU AQYRAZFR EQR QG VCAA.

— TQFFU GVQYRAMYT

200. HMFLQKPWZ SCGG OPUPW KBXP KJP
LGBHP MR DMMXZ. EMQ HBO'K ZKBON MO
B RGMLLE NCZX KM WPBHJ B JCAJ ZJPGR.

— ZBF PSCOA

201. K YKZ XAJPAQ PF RPLA YKLPCT K
OKLA QPDM KRR DMA YAFD PCTXAZPACDF
KCZ MKJPCT FSEASCA FPD SC PD.

— ZKCPARRA FDAAR

202. RJW VWBYEC RJWVW BVW YE ZWK
ZWABXW NEXQRQPQBCY QY RJBR QR QY
REE AHPJ RVEHMXW RE NHR ABFWHN EC
RKE ZBPWY.   — ABHVWWC AHVNJD

203. PFQT L PBX CWJPLTC ZN, L BRPBUX
PBTYQK YJ DQ XJSQJTQ. TJP L WQBRLIQ L
XFJZRK FBHQ DQQT SJWQ XNQGLELG.

— RLRU YJSRLT

204. CJ NXK Y'L XO JSRMMXCRQ CMJPP
VWRO KJH WXSR ORSRM RSRO NRRO LR
UHXMQ X AMYQUR YN DXCROCPK HOTXYM.

— CYOX TRK

205. OUH LHTMBG YLTGEJTLHGOM TGE
WUZDELHG YHO TDBGY MB FHDD ZM OUTO
OUHR UTQH T WBKKBG HGHKR.

— MTK DHQHGMBG

206. YPMEPM PJ WM TXDHC GH NGVC JTC
PRPECWM PKPFEH. WM KGSC HPMH, "WPM
G TPBC JTC CLBCNXYC, YNCPHC?"

— TCLLM MXDLAWPL

207. OH COH W DCL LC LZCFWU
HYMUCR. MG ML OHNHR'L GCN ZMF,
OH'Y AH OWLXZMRQ LHDHEMUMCR AT
XWRYDHDMQZL.   — FMDLCR AHNDH

208. FR JUX SUT'E WLGS ECL TLYBHGHLW,
JUX'WL XTFTRUWOLS. FR JUX SU WLGS
ECL TLYBHGHLW, JUX'WL OFBFTRUWOLS.

— OGWM EYGFT

209. W MLIU NUCULHUN HMWD ULXHMJZXT
JWHM TG JZXND. WTLVWYU JMLH W JZBRN
MLIU NZYU JWHM TG CWXU-PXULHMWYV
CWDHD.   — QMLXRWU DMUUY

210. NPOZ MPCNVBHELJ EL ARPAHR KGP
OBV'S KNESR EVSRNTERKEVY ARPAHR
KGP OBV'S SBHZ QPN ARPAHR KGP OBV'S
NRBU.   — QNBVZ IBAAB

211. XGWC FPQ TCARPHGK. YTZ AN PC
PYUUCTD FG HC FYXX, ZCHGTYAK, YTZ
ZCWYDFYFATR, AF OAXX HC FPYF LJVP
CYDACK. —LYC OCDF

212. RMANA SX XJ BZEM TJYYZRSJF SF
RMA GSN FJC RMGR SD SR CANAF'R DJN
JZN YZFKX, RMANA CJZYQ PA FJ TYGEA RJ
TZR SR GYY. —NJPANR JNPAF

213. EUA YHUJ EUA'KQ SH ZUGQ JBQH EUA
RMH'F OMZZ MVZQQX NQRMAVQ KQMZSFE
SV OSHMZZE NQFFQK FBMH EUAK CKQMDV.
—CK. VQAVV

214. TDTPHLSRYE RA OSFYERYE. UTVUMT
FPT LFJRYE LSTRP OVQTKRFYA ATPRVCAMH
FYK LST UVMRLRORFYA FA F XVJT.
—BRMM PVETPA

215. QBFPFZU FL COLN. OWW NTY MT
FL LPOBC OP O KWOZV LJCCP TR EOECB
YZPFW MBTEL TR KWTTM RTBX TZ NTYB
RTBCJCOM. —UCZC RTQWCB

216. MKR'CA WQSWMF W QNJJQA
XNFWYYKNHJNHO NH YACFKH ZABWRFA
MKR BWH'J ZA JPA AXNJAX AFFAHBA KE
MKRCFAQE. —VAQ ZCKKLF

217. FGMJ ESXFB CJ GTMGTGHJFZ
DKVVGJO GM STFZ EJ ASXFB CJ CSOT
KH HDJ KPJ SM JGPDHZ KTB POKBXKFFZ
KVVOSKAD JGPDHJJT.   —NKOR HEKGT

218. XTA SAJQML NMQX WAMWHA WHJC
ZMHD UQ XM FAJS RHMXTAQ XTAC FMYHK
LMX PA RJYZTX KAJK UL MXTASFUQA.
                         —SMZAS QUNML

219. BRGRF CFOJBCGRHQB GQF DFQFCS
KHCJRJLJGEB XZHBF VGQYFBR BFLQFR
KQFWFERB RZFD NQHD QTEEJEO NHQ G
ZJOZFQ HNNJLF.   —VFEEJB DJCCFQ

220. HTWE UP ADALSETUMC UO WM
UJJQOUVM WMF MVETUMC ARUOEO? UM
ETWE KWOA, U FAPUMUEAJS VDALNWUF
PVL BS KWLNAE.   —HVVFS WJJAM

221. BRSC HEY ASS J XJNNTSP LEYFOS
BJOWTCM PEBC VRS AVNSSV, VRS ECS
VRJV'A J QSB AVSFA JRSJP TA VRS ECS
VRJV'A XJP.   —RSOSC NEBOJCP

222. R PUDBQENM OBNRBJB EPBLB RQ
HOQUNAEBNM DUEPRDK NRWB KURDK EU
OBF SREP H KUUF OUUW. UL H CLRBDF
SPU'Q LBHF UDB.   —YPMNNRQ FRNNBL

223. PTRVRORZ QAG CZR CLERK YU QAG
HCV KA C DAS, NRBB NTRF, "HRZNCYVBQ,
Y HCV!" —NTRV WRN SGLQ CVK BRCZV TAP
NA KA YN.   —NTRAKAZR ZAALRORBN

224. LO NZH TAFZQKA GZ XLKA HJ
FYZPLBX, CTLBPLBX, UBC QZKLBX, NZH
CZB'G USGHUQQN QLKA QZBXAT. LG MHFG
OAAQF GWUG EUN.   —SQAYABG OTAHC

225. VUR CVVK JDMUC FQVOJ CRJJMUC
VEKRY MZ AVO KMZHVGRY AVO FYR TVYR
MUJRYRZJMUC JDFU TVZJ WRVWER AVO
TRRJ.   —ERR TFYGMU

226. CRP PBVXVHD OPYPXOJ LNVFC LJ
HFBR VX PBVXVHSJCJ LJ CRP KPLCRPZ
OVPJ VX KPLCRPZ QVZPBLJCPZJ.
          —UPLX-YLFE WLFQQHLXX

227. O ZUPV U LOBHRV HZORALAHZM:
XORR SZUJ'L VBHJM, VBHJM SZUJ'L XNRR,
UEQ LFKUJFZ SZVKV OJ OJFZVL.
          —UROFV KAALVPVRJ RAEYSAKJZ

228. GJFFDHBUU DU XEPT CBHNDUN
NBQQDHO XEP DN VEH'N GPTN JHC NGBH
GJADHO GDR ZJNZG GDU GJHC DH NGB
CTDQQ.   —MEGHHX ZJTUEH

229. OJD FBJQ OJD'LG VGEU E RJJU TJJF QWGB OJD PDVB PWG NEXP KERG EBU HGGN E NSPPNG EX SH OJD WELG NJXP E HVSGBU. —KEDN XQGGBGO

230. MCQ XG MCVD MV NTZY NB FBK MV'LV GTXK NB AV ELTQXDF, AON MCVD FBK NTZYG NB OG, MV'LV GUCXIBECLVDXU? —ZXZQ NBRZXD

231. BSY VYHLBS AE W EMVZ OSAPVR XY RMKYNBVU JKAJAKBMAHWBY BA BSY YHRPKWHNY AE BSY SPZWH XVWRRYK. —WVEKYR SMBNSNANC

232. FMGU YB L WYTU. PEC KXUCXUT YC YB VMYJV CM KLTH OMET XULTC MT PETJ SMKJ OMET XMEBU, OME RLJ JUGUT CUFF. —ZMLJ RTLKWMTS

233. ZBU KUYZ NEAU XJA BPWJNBJVQACS CY ZJ XJARUZ SKJEZ PJEA JOV KJQP SVQ RUZ CVZUAUYZUQ CV YJLUJVU UGYU'Y. —RJJQLSV SNU

234. SBPQBC RMQ VZ ESUSTFC QD TCVBK OSGC UXCZVGCBN ZMQHFG QB BQ SEEQHBN TC SFFQRCG NQ GQ NMC YQT. —GQHKFSZ SGSOZ

235. FBHEMFW DQF YAAT QF QGWJLAFH WBMFW PMYA HSB TABTPA SEB QGAF'H ZJGA SEQH HEAR'GA QGWJMFW QCBJH.

—B.Q. CQHHMZHQ

236. VRZ VP JTZ QUDQRJQFZK VP EZLRF ULKVMUZMXC LK JTQJ VRZ LK YVRKJQRJXC NQGLRF ZSYLJLRF ULKYVDZMLZK.

—Q.Q. NLXRZ

237. DTTLCZQQ ETUCKWGP LJG LVT VTNPL LJKWHP ZCTOL ZUGNKEZ: KL KP RKTQGWEG FOWELOZLGS CB ETUUKLLGG UGGLKWHP.

—HGTNHG D. VKQQ

238. EVGO EWQ MCO DHWEE UE CWHR OGAMQ, WKY EVGO EWQ MCO DHWEE UE CWHR RPHH, JPM U EWQ MCO DHWEE UE MVV JUD.

—DOVLDO NWLHUK

239. OGP MCC D KGX GU MVDZX WPOM RHXB TPVE RGVCL, EPX OGP BDZTKO CQCZ MCC D MVDZX RGVDL RHXB D TPVE WPO.

—CZHSD NGLW

240. YUFQF'H WA QFMHAW YA RF YUF QBSUFHY PMW BW YUF SFPFYFQL. LAZ SMW'Y TA PZSU RZHBWFHH JQAP YUFQF.

—SANAWFN HMWTFQH

48

241. VMGF'XG KAQBOOF HDPG WR YAVM
VMG RGTKGHV DKKAHG HDPRWVGT. AK AV
PBJGU B PAUVBJG, AV EOBPGU BQDVMGT
HDPRWVGT.   — PAOVDQ EGTOG

242. H OMNTBM DS GLAHD DWGD H GA
ASOM DWGR NHNDQ-DKS, MEMR HN DWGD
LSMB AGZM AQ BSRB HXXMCHDHAGDM.
                          — RGRJQ GBDSO

243. YPFL E CGXLO WEL BGWQVEALD HPEH
E CGXLO VEKC PED LG PFEUH, AH AD E
QUFHHC BFUHEAL DAOL HPEH DPF PED
PAD.   — OFGUOF K. QUFLHABF

244. WSAUA JUA VAPAOWF KGBBGQO
EQQDV GO JKAUGLJO BGEUJUGAV, EZW
WSA QOA FQZ HJOW WQ UAJN GV JBHJFV
QZW.   — WQK KJVVQO

245. UDN TX AGXJ U HGKLNQ. TJ'X
JYJUCCB TQQNCNRUHJ. GHCNXX, YM
FYGQXN, BYG'QN U LYJJCN YM ZTHN.
                          — AYUH FYCCTHX

246. GT WTUPZZPLUVGZ WC G RGT EMK
UGJPC RKOP EKONC UMGT TPLPCCGOX UK
UPZZ RKOP UMGT MP JTKEC.
                — NEWSMU N. PWCPTMKEPO

49

247. UPLGAQAN CKH ELC WA OHNA KD,
WA OHNA KD GPJO — GPLG CKH LNA
ZNALZDHRRC RJVA KGPAN TAKTRA.

— MLEAO NHOOARR RKUARR

248. R BCCYP GY RH RHGBRA ZGWE
ECVHY CH WEP TVCHW CT EGY EPRJ RHJ R
EMHWGHD ACJDP ZRAA CH WEP NRQU CT
GW.   — DVCMQEC BRVK

249. PSL YEMLYP CEN PU AUWGKL NUWX
OUTLN BY PU MUKA BP UZLX UTJL ETA
VWP BP BT NUWX VUJQLP. — QBT SWGGEXA

250. KC PAV EHD JKQY PAV QBAR RXED
PAV'GY MAKBW, PAV HEB MA EBPDXKBW
PAV REBD — YOHYLD BYVGANVGWYGP.

— NXEGAB NDABY

251. K SBRBRHBS PEBT VEB FGTJOB QEUW
HYSTBJ JUPT. BZBSCUTB QVUUJ GSUYTJ
QKTLKTL "EGWWC HKSVEJGC."

— QVBZBT PSKLEV

252. COGAGZGD V OGRD RAPBAG RDFYVAF
UBD QTRZGDP, V UGGT R QKDBAF
VWEYTQG KB QGG VK KDVGS BA OVW
EGDQBARTTP.   — RNDRORW TVAMBTA

253. RUG'M VOOKUVFJ V YUVM WKUE MJD WKUGM, V JUKLD WKUE MJD AVFX, UK V WUUZ WKUE VGP LBRD.

—PBRRBLJ OKUNDKA

254. GYKKST NQT: CDTX FZSSYXQ NX NSS-XYQDWTH GTNXL XVW DNBYXQ WV QTW ZF WV QV WV WDT ENWDHVVG.

—GYPDNTS UTSKGNX

255. UPADX KOPRAWPDN AR MAYP OQDDADX T VPZPNPOJ; JEQ'GP XEN T MEN EH KPEKMP QDWPO JEQ TDW DEUEWJ AR MARNPDADX.

—UAMM VMADNED

256. MJUF BA MBFJ QSL HXC? MSLEW JUBP AFST KPSMBCK SC QSLP VJXAF BY QSL UAGXW WBPXVFBSCA ASHXMJXPX?

—XPHU RSHRXVG

257. KZBY ZR VYAAYO ANUM XYUAN, Z VYKZYLY, ZB EMKF VYWUCRY ZA ZR KYRR VEOZMP UMX VYWUCRY ZA NUR BOYRN QYUWNYR ZM ZA.

—UKZWY SUKDYO

258. M BT MUPN CNRJ UNZ. M BT CFPPMUC GWFPPD CNNH. M EBU BRTNLP KMP PKF ABRR BL JBW BL M EBU PKWNZ PKF ERXAL.

—ANA FPPMUCFW

259. FC FXDKHV ZEOP, "CXM BXW'D
EFXMWD DX EWCDKOWS GHJEMZH CXM
YVXJVEZDOWEDH." O ZEOP, "NMZD CXM
BEOD."   —NMPC DHWMDE

260. LKTUT'W QC PXWEQTWW OEMT WKCZ
PXWEQTWW, PXL LKTUT JUT WTYTUJO
PXWEQTWWTW OEMT JSSCXQLEQA.
                    —NJYEN OTLLTUBJQ

261. JWU YGSU JWGYV KPDLJ PUGYV K
SUXUPFGJO GC JWKJ MWUY ODL PDFU
ZUDZXU, JWUO JWGYQ GJ'C JWUGF HKLXJ.
                    —WUYFO QGCCGYVUF

262. ZSXBSH YPB HZVD VPUHH RHZGD
Z MZX DPBWGM WSMHUDVZSM YPX
LBBOCBBOD BWVDHGG DHF CBBOD VPUHH
VB BSH.   —G.R. CBXM

263. DVTST NJ E OTSB TEJB REB DC
STDASM USCY E PEJNMC RNDV E JYEXX
UCSDAMT: HC DVTST RNDV E XESHT CMT.
                    —GEPW BTXDCM

264. SYUSLG MV CWTV JP LPNH
TQWYKHVC, MVTSNGV JQVL SHV JQV PCVG
UQP UWYY TQPPGV LPNH HVGJ QPZV.
                    —OQLYYWG KWYYVH

265. MBL AJH PRXXKJC RQC PREJ SQJ PRQ
PKWJXRUOJ MBJQ K GRQ WHRL WKQAOJ
RQC PREJ HBSYWRQCW PKWJXRUOJ?

— GRXXKJ WQSM

266. K RSQN ZNQNH TNNZ CNSGJDO — ZJL
NQNZ MRNZ YA WSW XKZKORNW XKXLR
EHSWN S ANSH TNXJHN K WKW.

— CNXX XJFMJHLRA

267. MHH RTP TNN MWD FDHFND EWH
XZHE WHE MH LOZ MWD VHOZMLS TLD
ROBS PLYQYZC MTUYVTRB TZP VOMMYZC
WTYL.   — CDHLCD ROLZB

268. CW PWWA K OCWMXW-DOWB BJVUJKN
QVJ TVNBSMDZXW OKMEWJD. OYWH TVSMA
TKMM ZO "VP KPVP KPVP."

— BKSMK BVSPADOVPW

269. DPJ ZXHXZADV FR PMGXC KJACTO DF
KFNJ FCJ XCFDPJN OJJGO DF KJ SXODQV
TNJXDJN DPXC DPXD FR XCV FDPJN
XCAGXQ.   — P.Q. GJCZWJC

270. U HSNWDFUQ SZ U FUB LJD UWLUGZ
TMFMFEMTZ U LDFUB'Z ESTQJHUG ECQ
BMKMT TMFMFEMTZ JMT UOM.

— TDEMTQ ATDZQ

271. CMUQ P CLR L GPYYGU FPS, CU MLS
L RLQSHTV. PY CLR L KOPNFRLQS HTV. P
CLR LQ TQGZ NMPGS, UDUQYOLGGZ.

                       — RYUDUQ CXPEMY

272. E NJODMF XU REVH EC YHZ REFM
JCWFMHL XJC JCZ E RJB NLOBMHZ. BW E
BJEZ, "DHF WVV XH, UWO FRW!"

                       — HXW AMETEAB

273. S ASMEOEAM EA S DSK NQL
VEAULHZOA FKWJZSASKM MQEKBA STLFM
QEDAZJG SKV MQZK ASPA MQZD STLFM
LMQZO WZLWJZ.   — WZMZO DUSOMQFO

274. ZOPPSV RHV OT MJVX KCAQ CSP
DSRTTZRGVT RQV TC HQVK, MQOXYSVP,
RXP URSP GJRG GJVK WROS GC
QVDCHXOIV KCA.   — UVXXVGG DVQW

275. EXQYXCQ SE FZCD YZMLBSQJ, YXW
LQUD KAZQ SW SE ZFZQ — LQZ BXEW YZ
MTCZHXU QLW WL ULLR USRZ T BSNZP
JCSUU.   — QLZU MLKTCP

276. SMC XLGSCE RSZSCR GR AGBC SMC
YXO ZS SMC UZKSO PMT YGFCR NTNZGLC
ST CFCKOQTEO ZLE RSGAA LTQTEO AGBCR
MGJ.   — HGJ RZJXCAR

277. DGGX TGZZCAPTUQPGA OLGCWX YJ
UO OQPZCWUQPAD UO YWUTV TGSSJJ UAX
KCOQ UO LUFX QG OWJJH USQJF.
　　　　　—UAAJ ZGFFGR WPAXYJFDL

278. VWN VO BPN RVQB SRDVXBFWB
BPSWMQ BV XNRNRHNX FHVCB SWOFWB
EFXN SQ WNYNX EPFWMN JSFDNXQ SW
RSJQBXNFR.　　　　　—JVW RFXKCSQ

279. OVV NDHK CEKK OXMEN KVFFRHQZ
NMZFNDFW. CMW RDPKHYOV RVFOKEWF,
H'T KMMQFW ZM NM JP TFQNHKN OQP TOP.
　　　　　—FAFVPQ BOEZD

280. VRWGJ YL FOQFDL EFLBM GK F
WGMYPRW GS NJRNV. VFCB DGR BCBJ
VBFJM F HGAB FEGRN F SFNVBJ-YK-OFQ?
　　　　　—MYPA POFJA

281. ZFM TVS AFFD VDD EGK NKFNDK VDD
FA EGK EHBK HA EGK VJLKWEHXHSP HX
WHPGE VSJ EGK UMJPKE HX UHP KSFMPG.
　　　　　—OFXKNG K. DKLHSK

282. SXYHTMWCM OYXQJQKQ YB SXYHJXC
KLNK N KYVNKY JQ N BPDJK, NXW HJQWYV
OYXQJQKQ YB XYK FDKKJXC JK JX N
BPDJK QNTNW.　　　　　—VJTMQ SJXCKYX

283. VDVCJ OSQ'B LCVSO AB MU KV SKHV
MU BAQT AQMU MZV SCOB UY S RUOSQ
RAMZUGM SHBU YSHHAQE AQMU ZVC
ZSQLB. — PVCCJ HVRAB

284. C JWOM ZSFMY ACKJMR C JWR FCXM
FZ THVFCOWFM XZRMKFQ, LHF C WX FZZ
LHKQ FJCYUCYE WLZHF XQKMVS.
— MRCFJ KCFAMVV

285. E YEFFVPS YEL GUHMXS JHFQPD
UVG YVGDETPG. LH MGP VL DBH ZPHZXP
FPYPYKPFVLQ DUP GEYP DUVLQ.
— SMELP SPBPX

286. O'P TUZ E XFES PUKOF YZEX. O'KF
YZOSS LUZ ZNF YEPF MOHF O YZEXZFB
UAZ MOZN ZMFTZC-FOLNZ CFEXY ELU.
— MOSS XULFXY

287. YSAPQUBWHF MSQHWHKH WQ XAEWQL
OTWKJ VUVJP UK KOS MJQKH U VSAQN
UQN HJBBWQL WK UK KJQ MJQKH U
VSAQN. — MTUPBJH NUQU

288. K RGYTQF HJQ FYKAQ-HJYGMBJ CH
VOFGXCPF'Z CXF HYKQF GMH FKWWQYQXH
COOQXHZ GX SQGSPQ — KHCPKCX,
YMZZKCX, KYKZJ. — LCVQZ WYCXOG

289. ULJQJ HQJ UFV ULSRBP SR ULSP
KSTJ TVQ FLSGL FJ HQJ RJCJQ TZKKX
MQJMHQJA, HRA ULHU SP — UFSRP.

     —WVPL DSKKSRBP

290. FEGY ZYQP FR LQ J SROQHMKQMF
RV NEQNB JMP LJAJMNQY. MRT GF'Y JAA
NEQNBY JMP MR LJAJMNQY.

     —SHJNGQ JAAQM

291. FWLN MG NBY HYTLYN MG HOTTYHH
UK JUGY UH NM YWN QBWN VMO JUAY WKX
JYN NBY GMMX GUSBN UN MON UKHUXY.

     —EWLA NQWUK

292. F YLHLTHFE NQZMKT'Y TQGK XY ZQ
BKGXRKT JMXGBTKE QHYZKZTXJFGGW
QEJK, FEB HW JFT SQTKRKT FSZKT.

     —UKZKT BK RTXKY

293. OF OELAYC ZDY JBY MARX JBYF CBEG
AR VDACERC ZRX ZADVHZRYC SYQZPCY
RESEXF QZR HYZLY. —SPDJ DYFREHXC

294. VE TQKJX GYSXLQ LARLSQT ZLSL TK
LARLSQ, QDLH ZKNCB FL FNHVPM TQKJX,
PKQ TLCCVPM YBUVJL.

     —PKSGYP YNMNTQVPL

295. DTG YGOD RZM DE LGD Z JKJJM AO
DE YGL HEN Z YZYM YNEDTGN. DTGM RAPP
OGDDPG HEN DTG JKJJM GFGNM DAVG.

— RACODEC JGCBPGDEC

296. EZHRUO MVBD GVVS CBDUTQ RUCV
Z YVHRT RF XRST FTTRUO MVBD VPTU
CBDUTQ RUCV GVBRXXVU KBGTF.

— AVEU XT KZDDT

297. D ELOXF DYRQDZU DA MLO TLOXF
OZFUGKPRZF YLGKU TLFU, R PRC FRZTUG
ELOXF FGDHU MLO TGRIM.

— YDPTV VUFSUGQ

298. VCL ULMALV DB OJPJEHPE HU VD
SLLT VCL EFZU XCD CJVL ZDF JXJZ BADO
VCL EFZU XCD JAL FPNLMHNLN.

— MJULZ UVLPELG

299. ZNJ VWNU ZNJ'MK PKBBGWP NFA
UQKW CFF BQK WCSKD GW ZNJM EFCHV
ENNV QCOK "S.A." CLBKM BQKS.

— QCMMGDNW LNMA

300. RBXQOH QV GAMM. KSY VCAOL RMM
KSYF XQPA XFKQOH XS LS ZGRX XGAK CYX
CASCMA QO RVKMYPV NSF. — UROA NSOLR

58

301. UMXC X YHHS CMZBY XSXK MXS —
UMFB MF AXZS X YHHS CMZBY, MF DBFU
BHGHSL MXS AXZS ZC GFWHQF.

— KXQD CUXZB

302. KOUGU PJ QY BYPQK FK AOPSO NYC
SFQ JFN, "AUXX, P'W JCSSUJJECX QYA. P
WPHOK FJ AUXX KFVU F QFB."

— SFGGPU EPJOUG

303. U EQD CDNB FUEOVUZ UGXSJP NFD
VXGEP ADOXGD NFD NGSNF FUB U LFUJLD
NX MSN QNB MUJNB XJ.

— VQJBNXJ LFSGLFQEE

304. ES HFN YBCW WF GVQBPQ FCVH WTQ
KMEWEKP, LFC'W GVBH WFF VFNL, WFF
PFSW, WFF SBPW, FM WFF PVFY.

— BMWNMF WFPKBCECE

305. C UVTURKBG VL MUJ OVHN BQ
YJKLBH GUB XBBOL CM C LCPLCTJ CHN
MUVHOL BQ YVSCLLB.

— CXCH YCMKVSO UJKRJKM

306. YTER TB PGR EPPY LSTGF JELRA
JGPLSRA OSRARJB YPMR TB LOP EPPY
LSTGFB JELRA RJDS PLSRA.

— PBDJA OTYKR

307. VLYGY BCO PYJYG C RLXDU OK
DKJYDH NQV LXO FKVLYG BCO EDCU VK
EYV LXF VK ODYYT.

— GCDTL BCDUK YFYGOKP

308. MUADLU BV DFF UOQULCLYKUK QWDQ
LUENYLU OUA RFBQWUK DOP OBQ LDQWUL
D OUA AUDLUL BV RFBQWUK.

— WUOLJ PDSYP QWBLUDN

309. JUSW D TSZ'R BSAPL SJ EAYQ, CAR
WDRLYU AR RAWBNV DP YNSPZDLYT DPT
DXPSUWDNNV FMPPAPZ TSZ.

— WDXYN NSMARY USXAPRSP

310. OHJ ZWQPC UHPW QSHJG OHJPFWZN
TQULQDYCDCY NHP RJFG HCW MWWX GAQC
DC FDE UHCGAF MDGA Q LFOTAHQCQZOFG.

— QVZQD FGWBWCFHC

311. JYSJTO MHL QWM HJZM DP TDGC
FWXYL SXQW J RDSMY OD QWJQ SWMH
TDG TMYY, QWM HJZM SXYY FJCCT.

— VXYY FDOVT

312. YGD'A ZXNNT X CNBYCQ. JMFVQ
TGB'NQ SBPT ZXNNTFDC AMQ CNBYCQ,
AMQ GAMQN CBT FP GBA YXDZFDC.

— SBYYT MXZUQAA

313. ZEB SBXCBNZ QUKBX OY YUTBUVB
AEU ZGXVY OVZU L SOIIL LZ CUGX
U'NQUNJ OV ZEB TUXVOVP.

     —NELXQBY SOBXNB

314. KDUO YDSLQTUCOWDSU CTQ UWKHNJ
KDSDNDBRQU EQNWLQTQE WS OMQ
HTQUQSYQ DA C FWOSQUU.

     —KCTBCTQO KWNNQT

315. F BRY'G CHVHVLHC RYSLZES'J YRVH.
TZQ EZ SZM GTFYX GTH QTZUH "ERTUFYN"
GTFYN NZG JGRCGHE? —IJR IJR NRLZC

316. PKYQ OFQ JFLLSFEYO FLY JFUY
SM KYFTYM, VRP OH SO PKRMUYL FMU
ZSEKPMSME.   —BZSMP YFOPDHHU

317. SN LBCF ZSNABON FKHSXL NAKN HBO
FABOUJ XCRCD AKRC WBDC TASUJDCX
NAKX TKD ZSXJBZF. —CDWK EBWECTQ

318. UZXXHB XU GCA MHNQ UOMSG DCASA
QMJ UOAHV PH PSF PHV NAB GM RSAPZ PH
PSF PHV P NAB. —CAHSQ RAPSV

319. L NWDDLTH QZT PLDVQ NWC L
TRTD JLVVTH. UZTC L QTYY QZLV QB NG
XZLYHDTC, QZTG AKVQ WSBKQ QZDBU KF.

     —SWDSWDW SKVZ

320. HSHWBPAQB QAHE KJSH J PAAY TR
DKHZ, PFD TR ZAED GJEHE, DKJD'E OKHWH
TD EKAFCQ EDJB.

— GKWTEDAMKHW KTDGKHRE

321. JDG YBDA JDG EOP FGQQUBS E SDDN
QTUBS DGQ UBQD QTP GBUHPOXP ATPB
JDG FGQ DB SZUQQPO.

— NOPA KEOOJWDOP

322. ROLNMWPJQ PT M VJQORGSLH
WFPQK. PS CJL NJLHOQ'W TPKQ CJLG
QMZR, CJL'O FMDR WJ BMC NMTF.

— GPWM ZMR EGJVQ

323. G YGB XSDKQY ZUVBJX CVZU YQWS
SGWBSXZBSXX QH GBNZUVBT ZUGB US
KQSX QH UVX KVBBSW.

— XGYOSD AQUBXQB

324. XFT PLB BQUQO YF ZFEQ LYLMB, GTA
AZQ AOTAZ MR XFT PLB BQUQO NQLUQ
ZFEQ, RF MA'R LNN OMYZA.

— ELXL LBYQNFT

325. SPFAWAHE ZFNUMZJ MZ NUB XFPHC
WPFGLBL VFPB TWHLB UFSBL NUWZ NUB
TMPLN TFGP UFGPL FT W CMBN.

— CWZ ABZZBNN

326. ZCRF S ZBO B PSK, S ZBO DQQU. S
FRYRU NQX BF J-UBA. EA QTK EBF ZQVTK
CQTK ER VD XQ XCR TSNCX.

— UQKFRA KBFNRUGSRTK

327. ZNLFEUY PY PA MNMOYMOY WO
E WDON ZNLFEUY QCY MNMOYMOY NZ
QCNOY VCN QCEMG QCYA QWDG OYMOY.

— LNJYLQ ZLNOQ

328. YEM SYWSD PMV DWPMHVM HFPZ
HFV PJVMPKV FBKF DAFYYQ DHECVZH. PH
QVPDH HFVR APZ XBZC TELPBH.

— P. LFBHZVR SMYLZ

329. EX XQH MECCHX, ASWCT EWH ECNEDT
BEKPSKA GK XQHSW XSOXGHT. NQD BGK'X
XQHD UYTX AHX XECCHW BEKPHWT?

— AWHA WED

330. XEU POU RULCPDR KPONCKXCPO
XEVX V BVO REPDWZ EVNU CR XEVX
OPXECOA REPDWZ YU XVTUO XPP
RULCPDRWF.   — RVBDUW YDXWUL

331. EMXFNDXYNF MU WVUXEZ DAVYX
JDPMGB UFK DGS GVX JDPMGB RJMESNFG.
EMHF MU XJF VXJFN TDZ DNVYGS.

— SDPMS EVSBF

332. A UG ZGK FAZU EJCK BCZWNCWM
GXMVC AQ QNZW AZ CQ BGZW CQ AK AQ C
BCZWNCWM A LCZZGK NZUMVQKCZU.

      — MUECVU CXXBMKGZ

333. BXVA EDR'CV UDBA MAU DRK,
FDHVKXYAZ MPBMEF KRCAF RN — MAU
YK'F RFRMPPE KXV ADFVF DL EDRC
LCYVAUF.   — DCFDA BVPPVF

334. NKFQNKXKGF XOCF HK LYGJKNMOV. Q
XKDG, TYO ADG COAU QG TYON CFYXDAE
YGVT MYN CY VYGP. — HONF NKTGYVJC

335. BANCOCGX CX BQUKVBX OKQ
ASNZ BUARQXXCAS RAU JKCGK SA
BUQBVUVOCAS CX OKAYEKO SQGQXXVUZ.

    — UAWQUO NAYCX XOQDQSXAS

336. AJP'BR ZJDR Q DSYR FJX
ZRYJGQOSDI OKR TKSOR KJPMR.

   — FRMMSYQ MSLNMJD, QM MKR TQM
     XRSDI SDOGJZPYRZ OJ SDORGSJG
      MRYGROQGA IQVR DJGOJD

337. LPTUEK LNK TEXFUJ N LPEAQNQUT
ONE PFUE N DPKT-WXKNKOUT VXQVHNM PK
OEUTXA-ONET QNJ. — UNEC HXCJPK

338. ZJP TKMS RVS NSOL, ZJP OJ RVS
OBLVSL, KFO LBC TJFRVL UKRSX ZJP VKYS
RJ LRKXR KUU JYSX KHKBF. —DJKF XBYSXL

339. FOJT BTD JGTPS VTYPWJT MKTN
KPQT JEBTMKODA ME JPN; REEXJ
VTYPWJT MKTN KPQT ME JPN JEBTMKODA.

　　　　　　　　　　　　　　　—GXPME

340. SG JSCBT FSLB JRBTB, SJ RBFWT
JK HBCBCNBH JREJ JRBHB REXB EFYEAT
NBBG JSCBT FSLB JRBTB.　—WEVF REHXBA

341. KL MWSD JTDPRQF NKNR'Q ATUP TRM
GAKHNDPR, QAPDP'F T OWWN GATRGP
QATQ MWS YWR'Q ATUP TRM.

　　　　　　　　　　　　　—GHTDPRGP NTM

342. MJEMLB TK BKNUC EWMD LKS BMZT
LKS'T TK TCSXA. DWMD EZJJ DUMQW LKS
DK AUUG LKSC PKSDW BWSD.

　　　　　　　　　　　　—UCXUBD WUPZXYEML

343. YV SWL NWE'O JBEO OW JWCF, SWL
XBRQ OW JWCF OW QBCE QEWLAX UWEQS
HW OXBO SWL JWE'O XBRQ OW JWCF.

　　　　　　　　　　　　　—WANQE EBHX

344. QJSQ USDDGRK NWXYHRP NSV HGZR
QWFRQJRD KSC SBQRD KSC GP S UGDSNHR
QJR ZSQGNSV JSP WZRDHWWORK.

—TGHH NWPTC

345. SZK LOK SZROQ WLD CZLDEGO'S GL
RC SHW SL SKEE X YXP GHRJKH ZLT SL
QKS CLUKTZKHK.   —VRUUW AXEELO

346. ZOUFJ LJULQJ MOU ZOPVE ZOJS
EVUM JYJWSZOPVH XWJ X HWJXZ
XVVUSXVTJ ZU ZOUFJ UD NF MOU CU.

—PFXXT XFPKUY

347. CPL KPQO HTVDXDRT HXO VHKGOS DR
KCDJSVXPPU KPRYHDROXT FOY NZJJOYT
EZTY KPQO DR H NPM?   —EHF JORP

348. YM'K NKHJHKK MD CDJO S GHBKDE
MD SEQMCYEW CH KSQK FCYJH YE JDPH,
OBNEU, DB BNEEYEW XDB DXXYVH.

—KCYBJHQ LSVJSYEH

349. C LUFLDH YRRV L HBVVUD KQ
HECWBULZE TLZMD CZ PLHR C HRR L
HZLYR, FTCPT C LUHK YRRV TLZMD.

—F.P. QCRUMH

350. ME'D FSDE HMJG KONMZ. XQGT
BUS HMWG VB BUSCDGHP, OHH UP BUSC
OTTUBMTN QOVMED OCG NUTG.

—KGCCMHH KOCJUG

351. MAA VB TXHMSURC'K WGVJAQHK
KRQH BGVH HMS'K USMJUAURC RV KUR
DXUQRAC US M GVVH MAVSQ.

—JAMUKQ WMKFMA

352. HZSKBHM BP EZJD BJJBSGSBHM
SKGH HZS RDBHM BHYBSDN SZ G FGJSO
OZT CZTXNH'S RD PDDH NDGN GS.

—RBXX YGTMKGH

353. C XF SUG X LVBVGXECXS YVOXKWV
C TULV XSCFXTW. C XF X LVBVGXECXS
YVOXKWV C JXGV DTXSGW.

—X. NJCGSVR YEUNS

354. MZYUY EUY DYH HRPK JYEVMV BTUY
MT JY KUYEKYK MZES E MEPCRSO BES
ZEQRSO STMZRSO MT VEX.

—ATSEMZES VHRDM

355. UO PJ DUNNZUHX JN KXBZVUKR, BXP
U DUG PUCX ESZKS KJQNOX SX EZBB. SX
EZBB VX OQNX PJ NXFXGP. —OJKNUPXO

356. EPXYCEQY ECY: E WCBMGQY
BR YFH GTYENHTYHM XBNM PD YFH
GTWCUTQUWNHM YB YFH GYYHCND
PHOUNMHCHM.   —EN QEWW

357. YB DLR YD DQGW X MXAQOXZ
FWLMCVLMCM, WCH GCVL AWLOL XOL DC
VXMS JCCTD CM WCH AC NC YA?
                              —JLAAL VYNZLO

358. EWMF EJCMF OSM NMVSMTTMN,
PWMA MOP JS UJ TWJVVXFU. CMF XFKONM
OFJPWMS HJDFPSA.   —MGOAFM LJJTGMS

359. PQZ QYEWZMP PQLAH PS WLMHCLMZ
LM XSCE GZZOLAHM FQZA XSC JCP Y OSP
SG EZOYPLTZM SA PQZ PEYLA GSE QSBZ.
                              —NLA QCRRYEW

360. FY QAYZGYQ FY XZR YZBJDS
RFAYQQYQ XFYZB ZDQ XEUY BE MJDQ
FZVM BFY GZBBAYRR XZR SEDY.
                              —MAYQ ZVVYD

361. BWH DLB NA EHCXUXJH UNJQXQBQ NA
DEMQXJF BWH ODBXHJB SWXPH JDBMLH
UMLHQ BWH CXQHDQH.   —GNPBDXLH

362. VBSN AQEF XBDUBPKZ KBFNA ZQ HRK XQZH QOOSDK DBW NQZK HRKV SW HSVK OQF DRFSZHVBZ. —TQRWWA DBFZQW

363. CKGQXP QE WVMVTA GOV CMG ZD HVVYQXP C TCMPV PMZNY ZD YVZYTV DMZW KZNPOQXP. —MCTYO MQKOCMREZX

364. BQM BHDCLYM SFBQ KDOM SDOMZ FK BQMU PMB WYY MTVFBMA WLDCB ZDBQFZP, WZA BQMZ BQMU OWHHU QFO. —VQMH

365. SMBMDRPRAF NJP OKADMX SNJS OMAOBM ERBB BAAY JS JFWSNRFL KJSNMK SNJF MJTN ASNMK. —JFF BJFXMKP

366. OPMMVS ETS PJ NDSX QYHZ AZYEM OPXM EXM XEZZYN NEPJG ASTPX GY WDEXTS KVEWSJ. —S. BYJSKD WYJJOEX

367. EP'Y LMP PNU FMYP ELPUBBUHPXVB DMC EL PNU RMWBK, CXP E KM NVZU PM GLMR PNU BUPPUWY. —ZVLLV RNEPU

368. QLKQUL JLOLD UPL FK ZXHC EF ERNLD E CXJN, BXDPJW E SED, KD GLRKDL EJ LULHNPKJ. —KNNK OKJ GPFZEDHA

369. KORZW XK R ORZWGRWF AERA ARVFK YTT XAK HYRA, KUXAK YZ XAK ERZSK, RZS WYFK AY MYDV. —HRDO KRZSPGDW

370. GPAIA BL QM LNQIBLA LM XAENGBRNH GPEG BG BL FMIGP FEVBQS WA ND GM LAA BG. —WBQCZ VEHBQS

371. VATJJ P'KMPKQ BU NMYNZU VPP MNVJ PT VPP JNTMZ GPT NSZVABSL ZPW YNSV VP RP. —FJNS-CNWM UNTVTJ

372. SUP ZLA WLS CKLX SUP DGMH LVUPX DUAO QJHWWHW, VPX XKHS ZUEHJ L RPDXGXPQH UB WKGAW. —RLH CHWX

373. ZBYST CEZ JMTO M GSTL SB MBEYALV GMB'X GEWWMXSBX, CEZ WMB'Y SGMRSBL YAL XGLTT. —VEQLVY QCVBL

374. T NYRCCS XVA'O OUTAD T AYYX WMAJ VZ JOYYC. T'X WY URKKS QTOU WMAJ VZ HTAARGVA. —YCCYA XYEYAYNYJ

375. EMF LASH EOCF Y QLCYA KFYSSH DPNNFFWD OA NMYAJOAJ Y CYA OD QMFA MF OD Y ZYZH. —AYEYSOF QLLW

376. M DFNH LS HMUP TMW EFCUPNFT.
UPYU'T PCH M VNYFJNZ UC ZYJON —
HYMUMJD XCF UPN EYUPFCCQ.

—ECE PCSN

377. BJO KZSWA BZAHD AZOCY'B
PHUO COYCO, CZ KJD CJZFWA T XHTYB
XTVBFSOC BJHB AZ?   —XHMWZ XTVHCCZ

378. D VUEPJPHPDT PX D ODT CNU CPEE
BUYMEQ HFUXX JNDJ MFPBKQ CNQT NQ
HUOQX JU PJ.   —UXHDF EQZDTJ

379. QDYNPNE GTAR FYXNL BTX'C WHL
DTZZAXNGG GAFZOL RARX'C MXYQ QDNEN
CY SY GDYZZAXS.   —WY RNENM

380. TPNL ULPUFL XSFM RG XOLRC TFLLU.
FLKXQCLCT XSFM BORFL PXOLC ULPUFL
TFLLU.   —SFYLCX KSNQT

381. UQUYGNAU ZLB L KHYKNBU MA
DMXU. KUYZLKB GNHYB MB VLPRZMAW
PUDUQMBMNA.   —FLQMF DUPPUYELA

382. MACWABN AC PEFABN HBYXCC JEH
TSGTW SB STGHSY MACW, SBO GWXB AG
AC OACNHCGABN.   —OSKX PSFFJ

383. BJDZD KZD BCY VTXSH YR
HBKBTHBTQH: BJD VTXS MYN WYYV NA
KXS BJD VTXS MYN PKVD NA. —ZDF HBYNB

384. DNOAMN P KNS KZ LTQDVRC, P'C
RNWNM OVHHNR PR HAWN, DTS P'C
QSNJJNC PR PS V ONX SPKNQ.

—MPSV MTCRNM

385. GNL YFMDBH YZMR SAPFZALP TGMLP
ZFNGYNBENY TLH YZTXZ SAPFZALP
ALYNVZY.   —BDZFNX UDXUTLW

386. UKE'P VELN NKJO EVXWTAKO QTKFV
WOBFF XF WOVVEVO — TXF QBPVO AXGG
XF TXWTVO, PKK.   —VLBE VFBO

387. T QYC BAKEU NP'U XA OKGP ENPA
NP OKUPU XAVPLPUV XA NXU DTL JKL T
DKYROP KJ FTCU.   —VXH TOOPA

388. JAG YRXS JHQG JY GBJ FHGJ UYYF
HT CAHXG SYM'EG CBHJHRK UYE JAG
TJGBW JY LYYW.   —VMXHB LAHXF

389. YCETMYXK FEYLKM CW XYFQEK'W
AYJ SP NYGCXU JSQ MSSG MCGK JSQE
TYWWTSEF TBSFS.   —YM USEK

390. N QDWT GD GVB QXKB NXC'G
CBLBKKNWA. XG'K GVB KGYMXT DCBK
GVNG CBBT NFF GVB NTJXLB.

— PXFF LDKPA

391. UPM GARU AN SVBVYO VR OAVYO TZ
EYC UPM GPEYGMR AN SVBVYO EQM OAVYO
CAHY.

— NSVZ HVSRAY

392. ZVKUK'Y AKHKU KARNTV ZFDK ZR QR
MXX ZVK ARZVFAT ZVMZ CRN GMAZ ZR QR.

— JFXX GMZZKUYRA

393. AGCZMJRY JRPZZW SJCEGHRY BL
HGR GKBDRGKZM — HGRW YRFRJ HBJY
HGR ZCEGHD KOO.

— JPZLG SBD

394. YK YB LDKKDT KN WEOD PNODU E
BWNTK XEG KWEG GDODT KN WEOD PNODU
E KEPP.

— UEOYU MWEXLPDBB

395. LD GPJOF PJFB FJO VJZAJOF
TN JSJZDFQWOP W PJF, JKAJVF LD
CYWOMWOP QJGMGAQJB.

— NZJM GYYJO

396. GHDK WHTR SARE WPZZRG. WPNK
NPYR P TRKKPDR PEG DRN VPWY NH JHQ
ZPNRC.

— TPCJ VZJ

397. "PFZD, CKDDR PFZD" ZYCR CYXDWS
PEQD ODDJ KXVRRDJ OS E OETPDWFX.

— CEZYDW OYRWDX

398. OB WPXWE ON QAJXWG, EKM VKCA
FK KFA EJN WEAOP EJOP LKFA OF WEA
HOQPJPG? — HOHG WKCHOF

399. KNZNCQEQXH QE J VNFQPV LNAJPEN
QK QE HNQKBNG GJGN HXG DNZZ FXHN.

— NGHQN UXCJAE

400. X EJYM KXGBMA KJTQM KJNM RWFO
FOA DJKFO X WFYM MYMN BOJDO.

— DFER SXQOMA

401. RM YTF NEEW EP CRPF, YTF BMHZFQH
BQF MEY RM YTF NBSW. — STBQCRF NQEZM

ANSWERS

1. In Vegas, I got into a long argument with the man at the roulette wheel over what I considered to be an odd number. —Steven Wright

2. My grandma started walking five miles a day when she was sixty. She's ninety-seven now, and we don't know where the hell she is. —Ellen DeGeneres

3. If a cop pulls you over and asks how fast you were going, a good thing to say is, "I don't know, I was speeding the whole time." —Jack Handey

4. It's hard for the modern generation to understand Thoreau, who lived beside a pond but didn't own water skis or a snorkel. —Bill Vaughan

5. You can say any foolish thing to a dog, and he will give you a look like, "My God, you're right! I never would've thought of that!" —Dave Barry

6. I'd much rather be a woman than a man. Women can cry, they can wear cute clothes, and they're the first to be rescued off sinking ships. —Gilda Radner

7. Police arrested two kids. One was drinking battery acid, the other was eating fireworks. They charged one and let the other off. —Tommy Cooper

8. You know you're getting old when you stoop to tie your shoelaces and wonder what else you can do while you're down there. —George Burns

9. Instead of working for the survival of the fittest, we should work for the survival of the wittiest. Then we can all die laughing. —Lily Tomlin

10. I stopped believing in Santa when I was six. Mother took me to see him in a department store, and he asked for my autograph. —Shirley Temple

11. You can tell a lot about a person by the way he handles these three things: a rainy day, lost luggage, and tangled Christmas lights. —Maya Angelou

12. Why do publishers use large print in books for children, whose eyes are excellent, and small print in books for adults? —William Lyon Phelps

13. If there are no stupid questions, then what kind of questions do stupid people ask? Do they get smart just in time to ask questions? —Scott Adams

14. God gave women intuition and femininity. Used properly, the combination easily jumbles the brain of any man I've ever met. —Farrah Fawcett

15. It is amazing how quickly kids learn to drive a car, yet they are unable to understand the lawnmower, snowblower, or vacuum cleaner. —Ben Bergor

16. I asked my Magic Eight Ball, "Is there a reason my Microsoft email program crashed?" It answered, "Outlook not so good." —Shawn Kennedy

17. Marriage is not merely sharing the fettuccine, but sharing the burden of finding the fettuccine restaurant in the first place. —Calvin Trillin

18. A railroad station? That was a sort of primitive airport, only you didn't have to take a cab twenty miles out of town to reach it. —Russell Baker

19. I love the Waldorf-Astoria. You know, I hear that from the doorstep you can see all the way to the Russian Tea Room. —Barack Obama

20. How does that phone cord get so tangled? All I do is talk and hang up. I don't pick it up and do a cartwheel and a somersault. —Larry Miller

21. It is more fun to talk with someone who doesn't use long, difficult words but rather short, easy words like "What about lunch?"
—Winnie-the-Pooh

22. In elementary school, in case of fire, you have to line up single file from smallest to tallest. Do tall people burn slower? —Warren Hutcherson

23. Men want the same thing from their underwear that they want from women: a little bit of support, and a little bit of freedom. —Jerry Seinfeld

24. The problem with cats is that they get the exact same look on their face whether they see a moth or an axe murderer. —Paula Poundstone

25. If it weren't for the fact that the TV set and the refrigerator are so far apart, some of us wouldn't get any exercise at all. —Joey Adams

26. You have to remember one thing about the will of the people: it wasn't that long ago that we were swept away by the Macarena. —Jon Stewart

27. The disparity between a restaurant's price and food quality rises in direct proportion to the size of the pepper mill. —Bryan Miller

28. I've been called the Laurence Olivier of spoofs. I guess that makes Laurence Olivier the Leslie Nielsen of Shakespeare. —Leslie Nielsen

29. The trouble with the dictionary is that you have to know how a word is spelled before you can look it up to see how it is spelled. —Will Cuppy

30. The odds of going to the store for a loaf of bread and coming out with only a loaf of bread are three billion to one. —Erma Bombeck

31. Natives who beat drums to drive off evil spirits are objects of scorn to Americans who blow horns to break up traffic jams. —Mary Ellen Kelly

32. A positive attitude may not solve all your problems, but it will annoy enough people to make it worth the effort. —Herm Albright

33. The one great thing about waking up early is not jogging or greeting the day. That's when they make the donuts. —Kathy Griffin

34. My husband and I are either going to buy a dog or have kids. We can't decide whether to ruin our carpets or our lives. —Rita Rudner

35. Life is like a movie. There aren't any commercial breaks, so you have to get up and go to the bathroom in the middle of it. —Garry Trudeau

36. Having to read a footnote resembles having to go downstairs to answer the door while in the midst of making love. —Noel Coward

37. Lots of people want to ride with you in the limo. What you want is someone who will take the bus with you when the limo breaks down.
—Oprah Winfrey

38. I was out on a date recently and the guy took me horseback riding. That was kind of fun, until we ran out of quarters.
—Susie Loucks

39. How come when you blow in a dog's face, he gets mad at you, but when you take him in a car, he sticks his head out the window?
—Steve Bluestein

40. Somewhere on this globe, every ten seconds, there is a woman giving birth to a child. She must be found and stopped.
—Sam Levenson

41. Give a man a fish and he will eat for a day. Teach him how to fish, and he will sit in a boat and drink beer all day.
—George Carlin

42. My dad said, "Marry a girl who has the same belief as the family." Why would I want to marry someone who thinks I'm a schmuck?
—Adam Sandler

43. Sometimes I wonder if men and women really suit each other. Perhaps they should live next door and just visit now and then.
—Katharine Hepburn

44. I wanted to be the first woman to burn her bra, but it would have taken the fire department four days to put it out.
—Dolly Parton

45. Organized crime in America takes in over forty billion dollars a year and spends very little on office supplies.
—Woody Allen

46. I am confused by the phrase "stop, drop, and roll." The "stop" part doesn't belong. That's just extra time for being on fire.
—Jon Friedman

47. Remember that as a teenager, you are at the last stage of your life when you will be happy to hear the phone is for you.
—Fran Lebowitz

48. Buddha didn't get married because his wife would have said, "What, are you going to sit around like that all day?"
—Garry Shandling

49. It may be true that you can't fool all the people all the time, but you can fool enough of them to rule a large country.
—Will Durant

50. Somebody complimented me on my driving today. They left a note on the windshield that said, "Parking Fine."
—Tommy Cooper

51. Men are simple. They can survive a whole weekend with just three things: beer, boxer shorts, and batteries for the remote control.
—Diana Jordan

52. Please return this book. I find that though my friends are poor arithmeticians, they are nearly all good bookkeepers.
—Sir Walter Scott

53. I feel sorry for people who don't drink. When they wake up in the morning, that's as good as they're going to feel all day.
—Frank Sinatra

54. Ancient Rome declined because it had a Senate. Now what's going to happen to us with both a Senate and a House?
—Will Rogers

55. I love Valentine's Day. When you're a kid, everyone gets a valentine. It's like, "To Tim: Nice pants. Love Scott."
—Mike Birbiglia

56. You hate your job? Why didn't you say so? There's a support group for that. It's called everybody, and they meet at the bar.   —Drew Carey

57. Old age is when you resent the swimsuit issue of Sports Illustrated because there are fewer articles to read.   —George Burns

58. The man who developed the SAT test has died. His car going ten miles per hour ran into a train going sixty miles per hour.   —Craig Kilborn

59. You can tell a lot about a fellow's character by whether he picks out jelly beans all of one color or just grabs a handful.   —Ronald Reagan

60. The only reason why we ask other people how their weekend was is so we can tell them about our own weekend.   —Chuck Palahniuk

61. A woman can wait for the right man to come along, but that doesn't mean she can't have a wonderful time with all the wrong ones.   —Cher

62. You can't smoke in Los Angeles restaurants, which is ironic considering you can't breathe the air outside them.   —Greg Proops

63. It is a curious thought, but it is only when you see people looking ridiculous that you realize just how much you love them.   —Agatha Christie

64. A man can be called ruthless if he bombs a country to oblivion. A woman can be called ruthless if she puts you on hold.   —Gloria Steinem

65. Weaseling out of things is important to learn. It's what separates us from the animals—except the weasel.   —Homer Simpson

66. I have made a lot of mistakes falling in love and regretted most of them, but never the potatoes that went with them.   —Nora Ephron

67. Makeup only makes you look pretty on the outside. It doesn't help if you're ugly on the inside—unless you eat it.   —Audrey Hepburn

68. There are about five subjects to write songs about, and twelve notes. For all that, we musicians do pretty well.   —Elvis Costello

69. I don't think there's intelligent life on other planets. Why should other planets be any different from this one?   —Bob Monkhouse

70. When I sell liquor, it's called bootlegging, but when my patrons serve it on Lake Shore Drive, it's called hospitality.   —Al Capone

71. Women complain about premenstrual syndrome, but I think of it as the only time of the month that I can be myself.   —Roseanne Barr

72. An hour of basketball feels like fifteen minutes. An hour on a treadmill feels like a weekend in traffic school.   —David Walters

73. Having children is like living in a frat house. Nobody sleeps, everything's broken, and there's a lot of throwing up.   —Ray Romano

74. If I cut myself shaving, sausage gravy comes out. That's why I keep a small pile of biscuits next to the sink.   —Drew Carey

75. All writers are vampires. They'll watch you when you're not even thinking they're watching and they'll slip stuff in.   —James Gandolfini

76. Every day I get up and look through the Forbes list of the richest people in America. If I'm not there, I go to work.   —Robert Orben

77. A study in the Washington Post says women have better verbal skills than men. To the authors of that study: Duh! —Conan O'Brien

78. Home computers are called on to perform many new functions, including consumption of homework formerly eaten by the dog. —Doug Larson

79. Hollywood is high school. TV actors are freshmen, comedy actors are juniors, and dramatic actors are the cool seniors. —Owen Wilson

80. I asked this guy if he had the time. He said he'd love to give it to me, but he wasn't sure he could make the commitment. —Carol Siskind

81. Never try to impress a woman because if you do, she'll expect you to keep up to the standard for the rest of your life. —W.C. Fields

82. Jogging is very beneficial. It's good for your legs and your feet, and also the ground. It makes it feel needed. —Charles Schulz

83. The only man who is truly free is the one who can turn down an invitation to dinner without giving an excuse. —Jules Renard

84. I always have trouble remembering three things: faces, names, and I can't remember what the third thing is. —Fred Allen

85. The real menace about dealing with a five-year-old is that in no time at all you begin to sound like a five-year-old. —Jean Kerr

86. Fashion matters considerably more than horoscopes, rather more than dog shows, and slightly more than hockey. —Roy Blount, Jr.

87. The biggest seller is cookbooks and the second is diet books—how not to eat what you've just learned how to cook. —Andy Rooney

88. If the English language made any sense, "lackadaisical" would have something to do with a shortage of flowers. —Doug Larson

89. I have found some of the best reasons I ever had for remaining at the bottom simply by looking at the men at the top. —Frank Moore Colby

90. The reason women don't play football is because eleven of them would never wear the same outfit in public. —Phyllis Diller

91. The flight attendant will always tell you the name of your pilot. Like anyone goes, "Oh, he's good. I like his work." —David Spade

92. Freedom is like drink. If you take any at all, you might as well take enough to make you happy for a while. —Finley Peter Dunne

93. I think we should just tip the government if it does a good job. Fifteen percent is the standard tip, isn't it? —Pat Paulsen

94. Cable TV sex channels don't expand our horizons, don't make us better people, and don't come in clearly enough. —Bill Maher

95. I could dance with you till the cows come home. On second thought, I'll dance with the cows till you come home. —Groucho Marx

96. Conversation between Adam and Eve must have been difficult at times because they had nobody to talk about. —Agnes Repplier

97. Democracy means that anyone can grow up to be president, and anyone who doesn't grow up can be vice president. —Johnny Carson

98. I have found the best way to give advice to my children is to find out what they want to do then advise them to do it. —Harry S. Truman

99. How is it that one match can start a forest fire, yet it takes a whole box of matches to start a campfire? —Christy Whitehead

100. People think of the inventor as a screwball, but no one ever asks the inventor what he thinks of other people. —Charles F. Kettering

101. My friend Larry is in jail now. He got twenty-five years for something he didn't do. He didn't run fast enough. —Damon Wayans

102. In a thousand years, archaeologists will dig up tanning beds and think we fried people as punishment. —Olivia Wilde

103. Florida's all right if you can keep from catching a sailfish and going to the expense of having it mounted. —Kin Hubbard

104. If you know your Bible and your Shakespeare and can shoot craps, you have a liberal education. —Tallulah Bankhead

105. Weather forecast for tonight: Dark. Continued dark overnight, with widely scattered light by morning. —George Carlin

106. I find it rather easy to portray a businessman. Being bland, rather cruel, and incompetent comes naturally to me. —John Cleese

107. Children are smarter than any of us. Know how I know? I don't know one child with a full-time job and children. —Bill Hicks

108. Music played at weddings always reminds me of the music played for soldiers before they go into battle. —Heinrich Heine

109. I went to a record shop and said, "What have you got by the Doors?" He said, "A bucket of sand and a fire blanket." —Tim Vine

110. When a man has a birthday, he takes a day off. When a woman has a birthday, she takes at least three years off. —Joan Rivers

111. Don't do anything silly like going outside during a hurricane to have sex. Tell your friends you did, but don't. —Dr. Ruth

112. Never be afraid to laugh at yourself. After all, you could be missing out on the joke of the century. —Dame Edna Everage

113. Light travels faster than sound. This is why some people appear bright until you hear them speak. —Alan Dundes

114. The difference between a tax collector and a taxidermist is that the taxidermist takes only your skin. —Mark Twain

115. There are three ways to get something done: do it yourself, employ someone, or forbid your children to do it. —Monta Crane

116. I'm astounded by people who want to "know" the universe when it's hard enough to find your way around Chinatown. —Woody Allen

117. America is the country where you can buy a lifetime supply of aspirin for a dollar and use it up in two weeks. —John Barrymore

118. An intellectual is someone who can listen to the "William Tell" Overture and not think of the Lone Ranger. —Billy Connolly

119. When you reach for the stars, you may not quite get one, but you won't come up with a handful of mud either. —Leo Burnett

120. The average man who does not know what to do with his life wants another one which will last forever. —Anatole France

121. I went to the thirtieth reunion of my preschool. I didn't want to go because I've put on like a hundred pounds. —Wendy Liebman

122. If anyone corrects your pronunciation of a word in a public place, you have every right to punch him in the nose. —Heywood Broun

123. This is my ultimate fantasy: watching QVC with a credit card while making love and eating at the same time. —Yasmine Bleeth

124. Your marriage is in trouble if your wife says, "You're only interested in one thing," and you can't remember what it is. —Milton Berle

125. If country singers Tim and Faith wrote a memoir about married life, would they publish it through McGraw-Hill? —Shawn Kennedy

126. Everybody is a genius. But if you judge a fish by its ability to climb a tree, it will live its whole life believing it is stupid. —Albert Einstein

127. An uncle of mine was a clown for the Ringling Brothers Circus. When he died, all his friends went to the funeral in one car. —Steven Wright

128. I doubt whether the world holds for anyone a more soul-stirring surprise than the first experience with ice cream. —Heywood Broun

129. Hosting the Oscars is like making love to a woman. It's something I only get to do when Billy Crystal leaves town. —Steve Martin

130. In my experience, if you have to keep the lavatory door shut by extending your left leg, it's modern architecture. —Nancy Banks-Smith

131. Getting an idea should be like sitting down on a pin; it should make you jump up and want to do something. —E.L. Simpson

132. A businessman needs three umbrellas: one to leave at home, one to leave at the office, and one to leave on the train. —Paul Dickson

133. I think Bigfoot is blurry. That's the problem. There's a large, out-of-focus monster roaming the countryside. —Mitch Hedberg

134. Being in therapy is great. I spend an hour just talking about myself. It's kind of like being the guy on a date. —Caroline Rhea

135. The cocktail party is a device for paying off obligations to people you don't want to invite for dinner. —Charles Smith

136. A good hockey player plays where the puck is. A great hockey player plays where the puck is going to be. —Wayne Gretzky

137. Except during the nine months before he draws his first breath, no man manages his affairs as well as a tree does. —George Bernard Shaw

138. What a terrible round of golf. I only hit two good balls all day, and that was when I stepped on a rake in a bunker. —Lee Trevino

139. I'm so fast that last night, I turned off the light switch in my hotel room and was in bed before the room was dark. —Muhammad Ali

140. Be who you are and say what you feel because those who mind don't matter and those who matter don't mind. —Dr. Seuss

141. That men do not learn very much from the lessons of history is the most important of all the lessons that history has to teach. —Aldous Huxley

142. Last week I saw my psychiatrist. I told him, "Doc, I keep thinking I'm a dog." He told me to get off his couch. —Rodney Dangerfield

143. Inflation is when you pay fifteen dollars for the ten-dollar haircut you used to get for five dollars when you had hair. —Sam Ewing

144. Don't put off for tomorrow what you can do today, because if you enjoy it today, you can do it again tomorrow. —James Michener

145. At the age of four with paper hats and wooden swords, we're all generals. Only some of us never grow out of it. —Peter Ustinov

146. I pretty much try to stay in a constant state of confusion just because of the expression it leaves on my face. —Johnny Depp

147. Anyone can do any amount of work provided it isn't the work he is supposed to be doing at that moment. —Robert Benchley

148. The guy who invented the first wheel was an idiot. The guy who invented the other three, he was a genius. —Sid Caesar

149. Dancing is wonderful training for girls. It's the first way they learn to guess what a man is going to do before he does it. —Christopher Morley

150. I want to go on the record and say I have never urinated in public. But the night is still young. —Amy Poehler

151. When I get a headache, I do what it says on the aspirin bottle: take two and keep away from children. —Roseanne Barr

152. Be careful when you walk on an Oriental carpet because you're stepping on somebody's psychedelic vision. —Timothy Leary

153. I lost my job. Well, I know where my job is. It's just that when I go there, there's this new guy doing it. —Bobcat Goldthwait

154. Friendship is born at that moment when one person says to another, "What! You too? I thought I was the only one!" —C.S. Lewis

155. Why should we take sex advice from the pope? If he knows anything about it, he shouldn't. —George Bernard Shaw

156. By working faithfully eight hours a day, you may eventually get to be a boss and work twelve hours a day. —Robert Frost

157. I'm all in favor of keeping dangerous weapons out of the hands of fools. Let's start with typewriters. —Frank Lloyd Wright

158. My grandmother is over eighty and still doesn't need glasses. She drinks right out of the bottle. —Henny Youngman

159. Many a man has fallen in love with a girl in a light so dim he would not have chosen a suit by it. —Maurice Chevalier

160. Today, it takes more brains and effort to make out the income-tax form than it does to make the income. —Alfred E. Neuman

161. There is only one immutable law in life: in a gentleman's toilet, incoming traffic has the right of way. —Hugh Leonard

162. Wikipedia is the first place I go when I'm looking for knowledge—or when I want to create some. —Stephen Colbert

163. Acquaintance: A person whom we know well enough to borrow from, but not well enough to lend to. —Ambrose Bierce

164. A cop pulled me over and said, "Didn't you see the stop sign?" I said, "Yeah, but I don't believe everything I read." —Steven Wright

165. God writes a lot of comedy. The trouble is, he's stuck with so many bad actors who don't know how to play funny. —Garrison Keillor

166. I love it when I have a nightmare. To me, that means I got my money's worth out of those eight hours. —James Cameron

167. Did you hear about the fellow who blamed arithmetic for his divorce? His wife put two and two together. —Earl Wilson

168. Only Irish coffee provides in a single glass all four essential food groups: alcohol, caffeine, sugar, and fat. —Alex Levine

169. April first is the day upon which we are reminded what we are on the other three hundred and sixty-four. —Mark Twain

170. Did you ever see that painting, the "Mona Lisa"? It always reminds me of a reporter listening to a politician. —Robert Orben

171. Kissing is a means of getting two people so close together that they can't see anything wrong with each other. —Rene Yasenek

172. If women ran the world, we wouldn't have wars—just intense negotiations every twenty-eight days. —Robin Williams

173. Middle age is when you've met so many people that every new person you meet reminds you of someone else. —Ogden Nash

174. A birthday cake is the only food you can blow on and spit on and everybody rushes to get a piece. —Bobby Kelton

175. Macbeth and Lady Macbeth stand out as the supreme type of all that a host and hostess should not be. —Max Beerbohm

176. You know there's a problem with the education system when only one of the three R's begins with R. —Dennis Miller

177. When you're thirty, you're old enough to know better, but still young enough to go ahead and do it. —Brigitte Bardot

178. When someone tries to hand me a flier, it's kind of like they're saying, "Here, you throw this away." —Mitch Hedberg

179. I used to compete in sports, and then I realized you can buy trophies. Now I'm good at everything. —Demetri Martin

180. On cable TV, they have a weather channel. Twenty-four hours of weather. We had something like that where I grew up. We called it a window. —Dan Spencer

181. When I'm not in a relationship, I shave one leg. That way when I sleep, it feels like I'm with a woman. —Garry Shandling

182. There are only three stages for a woman in Hollywood: babe, district attorney, and "Driving Miss Daisy." —Goldie Hawn

183. I have always liked older men. They are just more attractive to me. Of course, at my age, there aren't many left. —Betty White

184. Authors are judged by strange capricious rules. The great ones are thought mad, the small ones fools. —Alexander Pope

185. Being in the army is like being in Boy Scouts, except that the Boy Scouts have adult supervision. —Blake Clark

186. There's nothing you can really do to prepare to rock. Do you prepare to eat a delicious meal? Are you hungry? Then you're gonna eat it. —Jack Black

187. Every man is a damn fool for at least five minutes a day. Wisdom consists in not exceeding the limit. —Elbert Hubbard

188. As far as I'm concerned, "whom" is a word that was invented to make everyone sound like a butler. —Calvin Trillin

189. To me, the outdoors is what you must pass through in order to get from your apartment to your taxicab. —Fran Lebowitz

190. If seven out of ten people suffer from hemorrhoids, does that mean that the other three people enjoy them? —Sal Davino

191. There is just one thing I can promise you about the outer space program: your tax dollar will go farther. —Wernher von Braun

192. If you wonder where your child left his roller skates, try walking around the house in the dark. —Leopold Fechtner

193. Why does a woman work ten years to change a man, then complain he's not the man she married? —Barbra Streisand

194. Fall is my favorite season in Los Angeles, watching the birds change color and fall from the trees. —David Letterman

195. I'm from Canada, so Thanksgiving to me is just Thursday with more food. And I'm thankful for that. —Howie Mandel

196. My boyfriend was cheating on me with his secretary. I found lipstick on his collar, covered with Wite-Out. —Wendy Liebman

197. The two leading recipes for success are building a better mousetrap and finding a bigger loophole. —Edgar A. Shoaff

198. In tennis, the addict moves about a hard rectangle and seeks to ambush a fuzzy ball with a modified snowshoe. —Elliot Chaze

199. I sold my house this week. I got a pretty good price for it, but it made my landlord mad as hell. —Garry Shandling

200. Computers will never take the place of books. You can't stand on a floppy disk to reach a high shelf. —Sam Ewing

201. A bad review is like baking a cake with all the best ingredients and having someone sit on it. —Danielle Steel

202. The reason there are so few female politicians is that it is too much trouble to put makeup on two faces. —Maureen Murphy

203. When I was growing up, I always wanted to be someone. Now I realize I should have been more specific. —Lily Tomlin

204. To say I'm an overrated troll when you have never even seen me guard a bridge is patently unfair. —Tina Fey

205. The reason grandparents and children get along so well is that they have a common enemy. —Sam Levenson

206. Payday at my house is like the Academy Awards. My wife says, "May I have the envelope, please?" —Henny Youngman

207. We owe a lot to Thomas Edison. If it weren't for him, we'd be watching television by candlelight. —Milton Berle

208. If you don't read the newspaper, you're uninformed. If you do read the newspaper, you're misinformed. —Mark Twain

209. I have defeated this earthworm with my words. Imagine what I would have done with my fire-breathing fists. —Charlie Sheen

210. Rock journalism is people who can't write interviewing people who can't talk for people who can't read. —Frank Zappa

211. Love thy neighbor. And if he happens to be tall, debonair, and devastating, it will be that much easier. —Mae West

212. There is so much pollution in the air now that if it weren't for our lungs, there would be no place to put it all. —Robert Orben

213. You know you're in love when you can't fall asleep because reality is finally better than your dreams. —Dr. Seuss

214. Everything is changing. People are taking their comedians seriously and the politicians as a joke. —Will Rogers

215. Writing is easy. All you do is stare at a blank sheet of paper until drops of blood form on your forehead. —Gene Fowler

216. You're always a little disappointing in person because you can't be the edited essence of yourself. —Mel Brooks

217. Life would be infinitely happier if only we could be born at the age of eighty and gradually approach eighteen. —Mark Twain

218. The reason most people play golf is to wear clothes they would not be caught dead in otherwise. —Roger Simon

219. State legislators are merely politicians whose darkest secret prevents them from running for a higher office. —Dennis Miller

220. What if everything is an illusion and nothing exists? In that case, I definitely overpaid for my carpet. —Woody Allen

221. When you see a married couple walking down the street, the one that's a few steps ahead is the one that's mad. —Helen Rowland

222. I honestly believe there is absolutely nothing like going to bed with a good book. Or a friend who's read one. —Phyllis Diller

223. Whenever you are asked if you can do a job, tell them, "Certainly, I can!"—then get busy and learn how to do it.   —Theodore Roosevelt

224. If you resolve to give up smoking, drinking, and loving, you don't actually live longer. It just feels that way.   —Clement Freud

225. One good thing about getting older is you discover you are more interesting than most people you meet.   —Lee Marvin

226. The economy depends about as much on economists as the weather does on weather forecasters.   —Jean-Paul Kauffmann

227. I have a simple philosophy: fill what's empty, empty what's full, and scratch where it itches.   —Alice Roosevelt Longworth

228. Happiness is your dentist telling you it won't hurt and then having him catch his hand in the drill.   —Johnny Carson

229. You know you've read a good book when you turn the last page and feel a little as if you have lost a friend.   —Paul Sweeney

230. Why is when we talk to God we're said to be praying, but when God talks to us, we're schizophrenic?   —Lily Tomlin

231. The length of a film should be directly proportionate to the endurance of the human bladder.   —Alfred Hitchcock

232. Love is a fire. But whether it is going to warm your heart or burn down your house, you can never tell.   —Joan Crawford

233. The best cure for hypochondria is to forget about your own body and get interested in someone else's.   —Goodman Ace

234. Anyone who is capable of being made president should on no account be allowed to do the job.   —Douglas Adams

235. Nothing can keep an argument going like two people who aren't sure what they're arguing about.   —O.A. Battista

236. One of the advantages of being disorderly is that one is constantly making exciting discoveries.   —A.A. Milne

237. Football combines the two worst things about America: it is violence punctuated by committee meetings.   —George F. Will

238. Some say the glass is half empty, and some say the glass is half full, but I say the glass is too big.   —George Carlin

239. You see a lot of smart guys with dumb women, but you hardly ever see a smart woman with a dumb guy.   —Erica Jong

240. There's no reason to be the richest man in the cemetery. You can't do much business from there.   —Colonel Sanders

241. They've finally come up with the perfect office computer. If it makes a mistake, it blames another computer.   —Milton Berle

242. I refuse to admit that I am more than fifty-two, even if that does make my sons illegitimate.   —Nancy Astor

243. When a young man complains that a young lady has no heart, it is a pretty certain sign that she has his.   —George D. Prentice

244. There are seventy million books in American libraries, but the one you want to read is always out. —Tom Masson

245. Age is just a number. It's totally irrelevant. Unless, of course, you're a bottle of wine. —Joan Collins

246. An intellectual is a man who takes more words than necessary to tell more than he knows. —Dwight D. Eisenhower

247. Whatever you may be sure of, be sure of this—that you are dreadfully like other people. —James Russell Lowell

248. A moose is an animal with horns on the front of his head and a hunting lodge wall on the back of it. —Groucho Marx

249. The safest way to double your money is to fold it over once and put it in your pocket. —Kin Hubbard

250. If you act like you know what you're doing, you can do anything you want—except neurosurgery. —Sharon Stone

251. I remember when the candle shop burned down. Everyone stood around singing "Happy Birthday." —Steven Wright

252. Whenever I hear anyone arguing for slavery, I feel a strong impulse to see it tried on him personally. —Abraham Lincoln

253. Don't approach a goat from the front, a horse from the back, or a fool from any side. —Yiddish proverb

254. Middle age: when pulling an all-nighter means not having to get up to go to the bathroom. —Michael Feldman

255. Being president is like running a cemetery; you've got a lot of people under you and nobody is listening. —Bill Clinton

256. What is with you men? Would hair stop growing on your chest if you asked directions somewhere? —Erma Bombeck

257. Life is better than death, I believe, if only because it is less boring and because it has fresh peaches in it. —Alice Walker

258. I am into golf now. I am getting pretty good. I can almost hit the ball as far as I can throw the clubs. —Bob Ettinger

259. My mother said, "You won't amount to anything because you procrastinate." I said, "Just you wait." —Judy Tenuta

260. There's no business like show business, but there are several businesses like accounting. —David Letterman

261. The nice thing about being a celebrity is that when you bore people, they think it's their fault. —Henry Kissinger

262. Anyone who eats three meals a day should understand why cookbooks outsell sex books three to one. —L.M. Boyd

263. There is a very easy way to return from a casino with a small fortune: go there with a large one. —Jack Yelton

264. Always be nice to your children, because they are the ones who will choose your rest home. —Phyllis Diller

265. Why get married and make one man miserable when I can stay single and make thousands miserable? —Carrie Snow

266. I have never been jealous—not even when my dad finished fifth grade a year before I did. —Jeff Foxworthy

267. Too bad all the people who know how to run the country are busy driving taxicabs and cutting hair. —George Burns

268. We need a twelve-step program for compulsive talkers. They could call it "On Anon Anon." —Paula Poundstone

269. The capacity of human beings to bore one another seems to be vastly greater than that of any other animal. —H.L. Mencken

270. A diplomat is a man who always remembers a woman's birthday but never remembers her age. —Robert Frost

271. When I was a little kid, we had a sandbox. It was a quicksand box. I was an only child, eventually. —Steven Wright

272. I caught my wife in bed with another man and I was crushed. So I said, "Get off me, you two!" —Emo Philips

273. A satirist is a man who discovers unpleasant things about himself and then says them about other people. —Peter McArthur

274. Middle age is when your old classmates are so grey, wrinkled, and bald that they fail to recognize you. —Bennett Cerf

275. Sunburn is very becoming, but only when it is even—one must be careful not to look like a mixed grill. —Noel Coward

276. The United States is like the guy at the party who gives cocaine to everybody and still nobody likes him. —Jim Samuels

277. Good communication should be as stimulating as black coffee and just as hard to sleep after. —Anne Morrow Lindbergh

278. One of the most important things to remember about infant care is never change diapers in midstream. —Don Marquis

279. All this fuss about sleeping together. For physical pleasure, I'd sooner go to my dentist any day. —Evelyn Waugh

280. Humor is always based on a modicum of truth. Have you ever heard a joke about a father-in-law? —Dick Clark

281. You can fool all the people all of the time if the advertising is right and the budget is big enough. —Joseph E. Levine

282. Knowledge consists of knowing that a tomato is a fruit, and wisdom consists of not putting it in a fruit salad. —Miles Kington

283. Every man's dream is to be able to sink into the arms of a woman without also falling into her hands. —Jerry Lewis

284. I have often wished I had time to cultivate modesty, but I am too busy thinking about myself. —Edith Sitwell

285. A married man should forget his mistakes. No use in two people remembering the same thing. —Duane Dewel

286. I'm not a real movie star. I've still got the same wife I started out with twenty-eight years ago. —Will Rogers

287. Journalism consists in buying white paper at two cents a pound and selling it at ten cents a pound. —Charles Dana

288. I worked the drive-through at McDonald's and tried out different accents on people—Italian, Russian, Irish. —James Franco

289. There are two things in this life for which we are never fully prepared, and that is—twins. —Josh Billings

290. This used to be a government of check and balances. Now it's all checks and no balances. —Gracie Allen

291. Part of the secret of success in life is to eat what you like and let the food fight it out inside. —Mark Twain

292. A suburban mother's role is to deliver children obstetrically once, and by car forever after. —Peter De Vries

293. My movies are the kind they show in prisons and airplanes because nobody can leave. —Burt Reynolds

294. If stock market experts were so expert, they would be buying stock, not selling advice. —Norman Augustine

295. The best way to get a puppy is to beg for a baby brother. They will settle for the puppy every time. —Winston Pendleton

296. Having your book turned into a movie is like seeing your oxen turned into bouillon cubes. —John le Carré

297. I would imagine if you could understand Morse Code, a tap dancer would drive you crazy. —Mitch Hedberg

298. The secret of managing is to keep the guys who hate you away from the guys who are undecided. —Casey Stengel

299. You know you're getting old when all the names in your black book have "M.D." after them. —Harrison Ford

300. Acting is hell. You spend all your time trying to do what they put people in asylums for. —Jane Fonda

301. What a good thing Adam had—when he said a good thing, he knew nobody had said it before. —Mark Twain

302. There is no point at which you can say, "Well, I'm successful now. I might as well take a nap." —Carrie Fisher

303. A lie gets halfway around the world before the truth has a chance to put its pants on. —Winston Churchill

304. If you want to please only the critics, don't play too loud, too soft, too fast, or too slow. —Arturo Toscanini

305. A highbrow is the kind of person who looks at a sausage and thinks of Picasso. —Alan Patrick Herbert

306. Life is one fool thing after another whereas love is two fool things after each other. —Oscar Wilde

307. There was never a child so lovely but his mother was glad to get him to sleep. —Ralph Waldo Emerson

308. Beware of all enterprises that require new clothes and not rather a new wearer of clothes. —Henry David Thoreau

309. From a dog's point of view, his master is simply an elongated and abnormally cunning dog. —Mabel Louise Robinson

310. You learn more about yourself campaigning for just one week than in six months with a psychoanalyst. —Adlai Stevenson

311. Always end the name of your child with a vowel so that when you yell, the name will carry. —Bill Cosby

312. Don't carry a grudge. While you're busy carrying the grudge, the other guy is out dancing. —Buddy Hackett

313. The perfect lover is someone who turns into a pizza at four o'clock in the morning. —Charles Pierce

314. Most conversations are simply monologues delivered in the presence of a witness. —Margaret Miller

315. I can't remember anybody's name. How do you think the whole "Dahling" thing got started? —Zsa Zsa Gabor

316. They say marriages are made in heaven, but so is thunder and lightning. —Clint Eastwood

317. It goes without saying that you should never have more children than car windows. —Erma Bombeck

318. Skiing is the only sport where you spend an arm and leg to break an arm and a leg. —Henry Beard

319. I married the first man I ever kissed. When I tell this to my children, they just about throw up. —Barbara Bush

320. Everybody does have a book in them, but in most cases, that's where it should stay. —Christopher Hitchens

321. You know you are putting a good thing out into the universe when you put on glitter. —Drew Barrymore

322. Education is a wonderful thing. If you couldn't sign your name, you'd have to pay cash. —Rita Mae Brown

323. A man seldom thinks with more earnestness of anything than he does of his dinner. —Samuel Johnson

324. You can never go home again, but the truth is you can never leave home, so it's all right. —Maya Angelou

325. Probably nothing in the world arouses more false hopes than the first four hours of a diet. —Dan Bennett

326. When I was a kid, I was poor. I never got an x-ray. My old man would hold me up to the light. —Rodney Dangerfield

327. Forgive me my nonsense as I also forgive the nonsense of those who think they talk sense. —Robert Frost

328. Our bombs are smarter than the average high school student. At least they can find Kuwait. —A. Whitney Brown

329. At the ballet, girls are always dancing on their tiptoes. Why don't they just get taller dancers? —Greg Ray

330. The one serious conviction that a man should have is that nothing should be taken too seriously. —Samuel Butler

331. Literature is mostly about having sex and not having children. Life is the other way around. —David Lodge

332. I do not mind what language opera is sung in as long as it is a language I cannot understand. —Edward Appleton

333. When you're down and out, something always turns up—and it's usually the noses of your friends. —Orson Welles

334. Retirement must be wonderful. I mean, you can suck in your stomach only for so long. —Burt Reynolds

335. Politics is perhaps the only profession for which no preparation is thought necessary. —Robert Louis Stevenson

336. You've done a nice job decorating the White House. —Jessica Simpson, as she was being introduced to Interior Secretary Gale Norton

337. Modern man drives a mortgaged car over a bond-financed highway on credit-card gas. —Earl Wilson

338. You make the beds, you do the dishes, and six months later you have to start all over again. —Joan Rivers

339. Wise men speak because they have something to say; fools because they have to say something. —Plato

340. In times like these, it helps to remember that there have always been times like these. —Paul Harvey

341. If your parents didn't have any children, there's a good chance that you won't have any. —Clarence Day

342. Always do sober what you said you'd do drunk. That will teach you to keep your mouth shut. —Ernest Hemingway

343. If you don't want to work, you have to work to earn enough money so that you won't have to work. —Ogden Nash

344. That married couples can live together day after day is a miracle the Vatican has overlooked. —Bill Cosby

345. The one thing you shouldn't do is try to tell a cab driver how to get somewhere. —Jimmy Fallon

346. Those people who think they know everything are a great annoyance to those of us who do. —Isaac Asimov

347. How come aspirins are packed in childproof containers yet bullets just come in a box? —Jay Leno

348. It's useless to hold a person to anything he says while in love, drunk, or running for office. —Shirley MacLaine

349. I always keep a supply of stimulant handy in case I see a snake, which I also keep handy. —W.C. Fields

350. It's just like magic. When you live by yourself, all of your annoying habits are gone. —Merrill Markoe

351. All of humanity's problems stem from man's inability to sit quietly in a room alone. —Blaise Pascal

352. Nothing is more irritating than not being invited to a party you wouldn't be seen dead at. —Bill Vaughan

353. I am not a vegetarian because I love animals. I am a vegetarian because I hate plants. —A. Whitney Brown

354. There are few wild beasts more to be dreaded than a talking man having nothing to say. —Jonathan Swift

355. As to marriage or celibacy, let a man take which course he will. He will be sure to repent. —Socrates

356. Abstract art: a product of the untalented sold by the unprincipled to the utterly bewildered. —Al Capp

357. If sex is such a natural phenomenon, how come there are so many books on how to do it? —Bette Midler

358. When women are depressed, they eat or go shopping. Men invade another country. —Elayne Boosler

359. The hardest thing to disguise is your feelings when you put a lot of relatives on the train for home. —Kin Hubbard

360. He dreamed he was eating Shredded Wheat and woke to find half the mattress was gone. —Fred Allen

361. The art of medicine consists of amusing the patient while nature cures the disease. —Voltaire

362. Mail your packages early so the post office can lose them in time for Christmas. —Johnny Carson

363. Acting is merely the art of keeping a large group of people from coughing. —Ralph Richardson

364. The trouble with some women is they get all excited about nothing, and then they marry him. —Cher

365. Television has proved that people will look at anything rather than each other. —Ann Landers

366. Middle age is when your broad mind and narrow waist begin to change places. —E. Joseph Cossman

367. It's not the most intellectual job in the world, but I do have to know the letters. —Vanna White

368. People never lie so much as after a hunt, during a war, or before an election. —Otto von Bismarck

369. Slang is a language that takes off its coat, spits on its hands, and goes to work. —Carl Sandburg

370. There is no sunrise so beautiful that it is worth waking me up to see it. —Mindy Kaling

371. Three o'clock is always too late or too early for anything you want to do. —Jean-Paul Sartre

372. You can say what you like about long dresses, but they cover a multitude of shins. —Mae West

373. Until you walk a mile in another man's moccasins, you can't imagine the smell. —Robert Byrne

374. I really don't think I need buns of steel. I'd be happy with buns of cinnamon. —Ellen DeGeneres

375. The only time a woman really succeeds in changing a man is when he is a baby. —Natalie Wood

376. I grew up with six brothers. That's how I learned to dance—waiting for the bathroom. —Bob Hope

377. The world today doesn't make sense, so why should I paint pictures that do? —Pablo Picasso

378. A politician is a man who will double cross that bridge when he comes to it. —Oscar Levant

379. Whoever said money can't buy happiness simply didn't know where to go shopping. —Bo Derek

380. Some people talk in their sleep. Lecturers talk while other people sleep. —Albert Camus

381. Everyone has a purpose in life. Perhaps yours is watching television. —David Letterman

382. Fishing is boring unless you catch an actual fish, and then it is disgusting. —Dave Barry

383. There are two kinds of statistics: the kind you look up and the kind you make up. —Rex Stout

384. Before I met my husband, I'd never fallen in love, but I'd stepped in it a few times. —Rita Rudner

385. Men should stop fighting among themselves and start fighting insects. —Luther Burbank

386. Don't envy your neighbor whose grass is greener—his water bill is higher, too. —Evan Esar

387. A guy knows he's in love when he loses interest in his car for a couple of days. —Tim Allen

388. The only time to eat diet food is while you're waiting for the steak to cook. —Julia Child

389. Airplane travel is nature's way of making you look like your passport photo. —Al Gore

390. A word to the wise ain't necessary. It's the stupid ones that need all the advice. —Bill Cosby

391. The cost of living is going up and the chances of living are going down. —Flip Wilson

392. There's never enough time to do all the nothing that you want to do. —Bill Watterson

393. Children really brighten up the household—they never turn the lights off. —Ralph Bus

394. It is better to have loved a short man than never to have loved a tall. —David Chambless

395. My agent gets ten percent of everything I get, except my blinding headaches. —Fred Allen

396. Dogs come when called. Cats take a message and get back to you later. —Mary Bly

397. "Home, Sweet Home" must surely have been written by a bachelor. —Samuel Butler

398. If truth is beauty, how come no one has their hair done in the library? —Lily Tomlin

399. Television is a medium because it is neither rare nor well done. —Ernie Kovacs

400. I love Mickey Mouse more than any woman I have ever known. —Walt Disney

401. In the book of life, the answers are not in the back. —Charlie Brown